CAMBRIDGE LIBRARY COLLECTION

Books of enduring scholarly value

History

The books reissued in this series include accounts of historical events and movements by eye-witnesses and contemporaries, as well as landmark studies that assembled significant source materials or developed new historiographical methods. The series includes work in social, political and military history on a wide range of periods and regions, giving modern scholars ready access to influential publications of the past.

English Seamen in the Sixteenth Century

James Anthony Froude (1818–1894) was one of the foremost historians in Victorian England, famous for his controversial 1884 biography of Thomas Carlyle (also to be reissued in this series), and for many works on England during the Reformation period. In 1892 Froude was appointed Regius Professor of Modern History at Oxford. This volume, first published posthumously in 1895, contains a series of lectures on the English navy in the sixteenth century which he gave at Oxford between 1893 and 1894. Informed by Froude's earlier research on the Reformation, the lectures focus on key leaders and events, as well as exploring the relationship between the growth of the English navy and the Reformation, and the role of Sir John Hawkins in exposing the Ridolfi plot to overthrow Elizabeth I. They provide many insights into the close connection between the court of Elizabeth I and the development of the navy.

Cambridge University Press has long been a pioneer in the reissuing of out-of-print titles from its own backlist, producing digital reprints of books that are still sought after by scholars and students but could not be reprinted economically using traditional technology. The Cambridge Library Collection extends this activity to a wider range of books which are still of importance to researchers and professionals, either for the source material they contain, or as landmarks in the history of their academic discipline.

Drawing from the world-renowned collections in the Cambridge University Library, and guided by the advice of experts in each subject area, Cambridge University Press is using state-of-the-art scanning machines in its own Printing House to capture the content of each book selected for inclusion. The files are processed to give a consistently clear, crisp image, and the books finished to the high quality standard for which the Press is recognised around the world. The latest print-on-demand technology ensures that the books will remain available indefinitely, and that orders for single or multiple copies can quickly be supplied.

The Cambridge Library Collection will bring back to life books of enduring scholarly value (including out-of-copyright works originally issued by other publishers) across a wide range of disciplines in the humanities and social sciences and in science and technology.

English Seamen in the Sixteenth Century

Lectures Delivered at Oxford,
Easter Terms, 1893–4

JAMES ANTHONY FROUDE

CAMBRIDGE UNIVERSITY PRESS

Cambridge, New York, Melbourne, Madrid, Cape Town, Singapore,
São Paolo, Delhi, Dubai, Tokyo, Mexico City

Published in the United States of America by Cambridge University Press, New York

www.cambridge.org
Information on this title: www.cambridge.org/9781108026666

© in this compilation Cambridge University Press 2011

This edition first published 1895
This digitally printed version 2011

ISBN 978-1-108-02666-6 Paperback

ENGLISH SEAMEN

IN THE SIXTEENTH CENTURY

WORKS BY JAMES ANTHONY FROUDE.

THE HISTORY OF ENGLAND, from the Fall of Wolsey to the Defeat of the Spanish Armada. 12 vols. crown 8vo. 3s. 6d. each.

THE DIVORCE OF CATHERINE OF ARAGON : the Story as told by the Imperial Ambassadors resident at the Court of Henry VIII. Crown 8vo. 6s.

THE SPANISH STORY OF THE ARMADA, and other Essays. Crown 8vo. 6s.

CONTENTS.—1. Spanish Story of the Armada—2. Antonio Perez : an Unsolved Historical Riddle—3. Saint Teresa—4. The Templars—5. The Norway Fjords—6. Norway once more.

THE ENGLISH IN IRELAND IN THE EIGHTEENTH CENTURY.

CABINET EDITION, 3 vols. crown 8vo. 18s.
POPULAR EDITION, 3 vols. crown 8vo. 10s. 6d.

SHORT STUDIES ON GREAT SUBJECTS.

CABINET EDITION, 4 vols. crown 8vo. 24s.
POPULAR EDITION, 4 vols. crown 8vo. 3s. 6d. each.

LIFE AND LETTERS OF ERASMUS. Crown 8vo. 6s.

CÆSAR : a Sketch. Crown 8vo. 3s. 6d.

OCEANA ; or, England and her Colonies. With 9 Illustrations. Crown 8vo. 2s. boards ; 2s. 6d. cloth.

THE ENGLISH IN THE WEST INDIES ; or, the Bow of Ulysses. With 9 Illustrations. Crown 8vo. 2s. boards ; 2s. 6d. cloth.

THE TWO CHIEFS OF DUNBOY ; or, an Irish Romance of the Last Century. Crown 8vo. 3s. 6d.

THOMAS CARLYLE : a History of his Life. With 3 Portraits. Crown 8vo. Vols. I. and II. 7s. Vols. III. and IV. 7s.

London : LONGMANS, GREEN, & CO.

ENGLISH SEAMEN

IN

THE SIXTEENTH CENTURY

LECTURES DELIVERED AT OXFORD
EASTER TERMS 1893-4

BY

JAMES ANTHONY FROUDE

LATE REGIUS PROFESSOR OF MODERN HISTORY IN THE
UNIVERSITY OF OXFORD

LONDON
LONGMANS, GREEN, AND CO.
1895

CONTENTS

ENGLISH SEAMEN

IN THE

SIXTEENTH CENTURY

———◆◇◆———

LECTURE I

THE SEA CRADLE OF THE REFORMATION

JEAN PAUL, the German poet, said that God had
given to France the empire of the land, to England
the empire of the sea, and to his own country the
empire of the air. The world has changed since
Jean Paul's days. The wings of France have been
clipped ; the German Empire has become a solid
thing ; but England still holds her watery dominion ;
Britannia does still rule the waves, and in this
proud position she has spread the English race
over the globe ; she has created the great American
nation ; she is peopling new Englands at the
Antipodes ; she has made her Queen Empress of
India ; and is in fact the very considerable phenomenon in the social and political world which all
acknowledge her to be. And all this she has

B

achieved in the course of three centuries, entirely
in consequence of her predominance as an ocean
power. Take away her merchant fleets; take away
the navy that guards them : her empire will come
to an end; her colonies will fall off, like leaves from
a withered tree; and Britain will become once
more an insignificant island in the North Sea, for
the future students in Australian and New Zealand
universities to discuss the fate of in their debating
societies.

How the English navy came to hold so extraordinary a position is worth reflecting on. Much
has been written about it, but little, as it seems to
me, which touches the heart of the matter. We
are shown the power of our country growing and
expanding. But how it grew, why, after a sleep of
so many hundred years, the genius of our Scandina-
vian forefathers suddenly sprang again into life—of
this we are left without explanation.

The beginning was undoubtedly the defeat of
the Spanish Armada in 1588. Down to that time
the sea sovereignty belonged to the Spaniards, and
had been fairly won by them. The conquest of
Granada had stimulated and elevated the Spanish
character. The subjects of Ferdinand and Isabella,
of Charles V. and Philip II., were extraordinary
men, and accomplished extraordinary things. They
stretched the limits of the known world; they conquered Mexico and Peru; they planted their
colonies over the South American continent; they

took possession of the great West Indian islands, and with so firm a grasp that Cuba at least will never lose the mark of the hand which seized it. They built their cities as if for eternity. They spread to the Indian Ocean, and gave their monarch's name to the *Philippines*. All this they accomplished in half a century, and, as it were, they did it with a single hand ; with the other they were fighting Moors and Turks and protecting the coast of the Mediterranean from the corsairs of Tunis and Constantinople.

They had risen on the crest of the wave, and with their proud *Non sufficit orbis* were looking for new worlds to conquer, at a time when the bark of the English water-dogs had scarcely been heard beyond their own fishing grounds, and the largest merchant vessel sailing from the port of London was scarce bigger than a modern coasting collier. And yet within the space of a single ordinary life these insignificant islanders had struck the sceptre from the Spaniards' grasp and placed the ocean crown on the brow of their own sovereign. How did it come about ? What Cadmus had sown dragons' teeth in the furrows of the sea for the race to spring from who manned the ships of Queen Elizabeth, who carried the flag of their own country round the globe, and challenged and fought the Spaniards on their own coasts and in their own harbours ?

The English sea power was the legitimate child of the Reformation. It grew, as I shall show you,

directly out of the new despised Protestantism.
Matthew Parker and Bishop Jewel, the judicious
Hooker himself, excellent men as they were, would
have written and preached to small purpose without
Sir Francis Drake's cannon to play an accompani-
ment to their teaching. And again, Drake's
cannon would not have roared so loudly and so
widely without seamen already trained in heart
and hand to work his ships and level his artillery.
It was to the superior seamanship, the superior
quality of English ships and crews, that the Spaniards attributed their defeat. Where did these
ships come from ? Where and how did these
mariners learn their trade ? Historians talk enthusiastically of the national spirit of a people
rising with a united heart to repel the invader, and
so on. But national spirit could not extemporise
a fleet or produce trained officers and sailors to
match the conquerors of Lepanto. ⌈One slight
observation I must make here at starting, and
certainly with no invidious purpose. It has been
said confidently, it has been repeated, I believe, by
all modern writers, that the Spanish invasion suspended in England the quarrels of creed, and united
Protestants and Roman Catholics in defence of
their Queen and country. They remind us especially that Lord Howard of Effingham, who was
Elizabeth's admiral, was himself a Roman Catholic.
But was it so ? The Earl of Arundel, the head of
the House of Howard, was a Roman Catholic, and

he was in the Tower praying for the success of
Medina Sidonia. Lord Howard of Effingham was
no more a Roman Catholic than—I hope I am not
taking away their character—than the present
Archbishop of Canterbury or the Bishop of London.
He was a Catholic, but an English Catholic, as
those reverend prelates are. Roman Catholic he
could not possibly have been, nor anyone who on
that great occasion was found on the side of Elizabeth. A Roman Catholic is one who acknowledges
the Roman Bishop's authority. The Pope had
excommunicated Elizabeth, had pronounced her
deposed, had absolved her subjects from their
allegiance, and forbidden them to fight for her.
No Englishman who fought on that great occasion
for English liberty was, or could have been, in
communion with Rome. Loose statements of this
kind, lightly made, fall in with the modern humour.
They are caught up, applauded, repeated, and pass
unquestioned into history. It is time to correct
them a little.

I have in my possession a detailed account of
the temper of parties in England, drawn up in the
year 1585, three years before the Armada came.
The writer was a distinguished Jesuit. The
account itself was prepared for the use of the Pope
and Philip, with a special view to the reception
which an invading force would meet with, and it
goes into great detail. The people of the towns—
London, Bristol, &c.—were, he says, generally

heretics. The peers, the gentry, their tenants, and peasantry, who formed the immense majority of the population, were almost universally Catholics. But this writer distinguishes properly among Catholics. There were the ardent impassioned Catholics, ready to be confessors and martyrs, ready to rebel at the first opportunity, who had renounced their allegiance, who desired to overthrow Elizabeth and put the Queen of Scots in her place. The number of these, he says, was daily increasing, owing to the exertions of the seminary priests ; and plots, he boasts, were being continually formed by them to murder the Queen. There were Catholics of another sort, who were papal at heart, but went with the times to save their property; who looked forward to a change in the natural order of things, but would not stir of themselves till an invading army actually appeared. But all alike, he insists, were eager for a revolution. Let the Prince of Parma come, and they would all join him ; and together these two classes of Catholics made three-fourths of the nation.

'The only party,' he says (and this is really noticeable), 'the only party that would fight to death for the Queen, the only real friends she had, were the *Puritans* (it is the first mention of the name which I have found), the Puritans of London, the Puritans of the sea towns.' These he admits were dangerous, desperate, determined men.

The numbers of them, however, were providentially small.

The date of this document is, as I said, 1585, and I believe it generally accurate. The only mistake is that among the Anglican Catholics there were a few to whom their country was as dear as their creed—a few who were beginning to see that under the Act of Uniformity Catholic doctrine might be taught and Catholic ritual practised; who adhered to the old forms of religion, but did not believe that obedience to the Pope was a necessary part of them. One of these was Lord Howard of Effingham, whom the Queen placed in his high command to secure the wavering fidelity of the peers and country gentlemen. But the force, the fire, the enthusiasm came (as the Jesuit saw) from the Puritans, from men of the same convictions as the Calvinists of Holland and Rochelle; men who, driven from the land, took to the ocean as their natural home, and nursed the Reformation in an ocean cradle. How the seagoing population of the North of Europe took so strong a Protestant impression it is the purpose of these lectures to explain.

Henry VIII. on coming to the throne found England without a fleet, and without a conscious sense of the need of one. A few merchant hulks traded with Bordeaux and Cadiz and Lisbon; hoys and fly-boats drifted slowly backwards and forwards between Antwerp and the Thames. A fishing fleet

tolerably appointed went annually to Iceland for
cod. Local fishermen worked the North Sea and
the Channel from Hull to Falmouth. The Chester
people went to Kinsale for herrings and mackerel :
but that was all—the nation had aspired to no
more.

Columbus had offered the New World to Henry
VII. while the discovery was still in the air. He
had sent his brother to England with maps and
globes, and quotations from Plato to prove its
existence. Henry, like a practical Englishman,
treated it as a wild dream.

The dream had come from the gate of horn.
America was found, and the Spaniard, and not the
English, came into first possession of it. Still,
America was a large place, and John Cabot the
Venetian with his son Sebastian tried Henry again.
England might still be able to secure a slice. This
time Henry VII. listened. Two small ships were
fitted out at Bristol, crossed the Atlantic, discovered
Newfoundland, coasted down to Florida looking for
a passage to Cathay, but could not find one. The
elder Cabot died ; the younger came home. The
expedition failed, and no interest had been roused.

With the accession of Henry VIII. a new era
had opened—a new era in many senses. Printing
was coming into use—Erasmus and his companions
were shaking Europe with the new learning,
Copernican astronomy was changing the level disk
of the earth into a revolving globe, and turning

dizzy the thoughts of mankind.   Imagination was
on the stretch.   The reality of things was assuming
proportions vaster than fancy had dreamt, and un-
fastening established belief on a thousand sides.
The young Henry was welcomed by Erasmus as
likely to be the glory of the age that was opening.
He was young, brilliant, cultivated, and ambitious.
To what might he not aspire under the new conditions !   Henry VIII. was all that, but he was
cautious and looked about him.   Europe was full
of wars in which he was likely to be entangled.
His father had left the treasury well furnished.
The young King, like a wise man, turned his first
attention to the broad ditch, as he called the British
Channel, which formed the natural defence of the
realm.   The opening of the Atlantic had revolution-
ised war and seamanship.   Long voyages required
larger vessels.   Henry was the first prince to see
the place which gunpowder was going to hold in
wars.   In his first years he repaired his dockyards,
built new ships on improved models, and imported
Italians to cast him new types of cannon.   'King
Harry loved a man,' it was said, and knew a man
when he saw one.   He made acquaintance with
sea captains at Portsmouth and Southampton.   In
some way or other he came to know one Mr.
William Hawkins, of Plymouth, and held him in
especial esteem.   This Mr. Hawkins, under Henry's
patronage, ventured down to the coast of Guinea
and brought home gold and ivory ; crossed over to

Brazil; made friends with the Brazilian natives;
even brought back with him the king of those
countries, who was curious to see what England
was like, and presented him to Henry at Whitehall.

Another Plymouth man, Robert Thorne, again
with Henry's help, went out to look for the North-
west passage which Cabot had failed to find.
Thorne's ship was called the *Dominus Vobiscum*,
a pious aspiration which, however, secured no success. A London man, a Master Hore, tried next.
Master Hore, it is said, was given to cosmography,
was a plausible talker at scientific meetings, and so
on. He persuaded 'divers young lawyers' (brief-
less barristers, I suppose) and other gentlemen—
altogether a hundred and twenty of them—to join
him. They procured two vessels at Gravesend.
They took the sacrament together before sailing.
They apparently relied on Providence to take care
of them, for they made little other preparation.
They reached Newfoundland, but their stores ran
out, and their ships went on shore. In the land of
fish they did not know how to use line and bait.
They fed on roots and bilberries, and picked fish
bones out of the ospreys' nests. At last they began
to eat one another—careless of Master Hore, who
told them they would go to unquenchable fire. A
French vessel came in. They seized her with the
food she had on board and sailed home in her,
leaving the French crew to their fate. The poor
French happily found means of following them.

They complained of their treatment, and Henry ordered an inquiry; but finding, the report says, the great distress Master Hore's party had been in, was so moved with pity, that he did not punish them, but out of his own purse made royal recompense to the French.

Something better than gentlemen volunteers was needed if naval enterprise was to come to anything in England. The long wars between Francis I. and Charles V. brought the problem closer. On land the fighting was between the regular armies. At sea privateers were let loose out of French, Flemish, and Spanish ports. Enterprising individuals took out letters of marque and went cruising to take the chance of what they could catch. The Channel was the chief hunting-ground, as being the highway between Spain and the Low Countries. The interval was short between privateers and pirates. Vessels of all sorts passed into the business. The Scilly Isles became a pirate stronghold. The creeks and estuaries in Cork and Kerry furnished hiding-places where the rovers could lie with security and share their plunder with the Irish chiefs. The disorder grew wilder when the divorce of Catherine of Aragon made Henry into the public enemy of Papal Europe. English traders and fishing smacks were plundered and sunk. Their crews went armed to defend themselves, and from Thames mouth to Land's End the Channel became the scene of desperate

fights. The type of vessel altered to suit the new
conditions. Life depended on speed of sailing.
The State Papers describe squadrons of French
or Spaniards flying about, dashing into Dartmouth, Plymouth, or Falmouth, cutting out English
coasters, or fighting one another.

After Henry was excommunicated, and Ireland
rebelled, and England itself threatened disturbance,
the King had to look to his security. He made
little noise about it. But the Spanish ambassador
reported him as silently building ships in the
Thames and at Portsmouth. As invasion seemed
imminent, he began with sweeping the seas of the
looser vermin. A few swift well-armed cruisers
pushed suddenly out of the Solent, caught and
destroyed a pirate fleet in Mount's Bay, sent to
the bottom some Flemish privateers in the Downs,
and captured the Flemish admiral himself. Danger
at home growing more menacing, and the monks
spreading the fire which grew into the Pilgrimage
of Grace, Henry suppressed the abbeys, sold the
lands, and with the proceeds armed the coast with
fortresses. 'You threaten me,' he seemed to say
to them, ' that you will use the wealth our fathers
gave you to overthrow my Government and bring
in the invader. I will take your wealth, and I will
use it to disappoint your treachery.' You may see
the remnants of Henry's work in the fortresses
anywhere along the coast from Berwick to the
Land's End.

Louder thundered the Vatican. In 1539 Henry's time appeared to have come. France and Spain made peace, and the Pope's sentence was now expected to be executed by Charles or Francis, or both. A crowd of vessels large and small was collected in the Scheldt, for what purpose save to transport an army into England? Scotland had joined the Catholic League. Henry fearlessly appealed to the English people. Catholic peers and priests might conspire against him, but, explain it how we will, the nation was loyal to Henry and came to his side. The London merchants armed their ships in the river. From the seaports everywhere came armed brigantines and sloops. The fishermen of the West left their boats and nets to their wives, and the fishing was none the worse, for the women handled oar and sail and line and went to the whiting grounds, while their husbands had gone to fight for their King. Genius kindled into discovery at the call of the country. Mr. Fletcher of Rye (be his name remembered) invented a boat the like of which was never seen before, which would work to windward, with sails trimmed fore and aft, the greatest revolution yet made in shipbuilding. A hundred and fifty sail collected at Sandwich to match the armament in the Scheldt; and Marillac, the French ambassador, reported with amazement the energy of King and people.

The Catholic Powers thought better of it. This

was not the England which Reginald Pole had told
them was longing for their appearance. The
Scheldt force dispersed. Henry read Scotland a
needed lesson. The Scots had thought to take him
at disadvantage, and sit on his back when the
Emperor attacked him. One morning when the
people at Leith woke out of their sleep, they found
an English fleet in the Roads ; and before they had
time to look about them, Leith was on fire and
Edinburgh was taken. Charles V., if he had ever
seriously thought of invading Henry, returned to
wiser counsels, and made an alliance with him
instead. The Pope turned to France. If the
Emperor forsook him, the Most Christian King
would help. He promised Francis that if he could
win England he might keep it for himself. Francis
resolved to try what he could do.

Five years had passed since the gathering at
Sandwich. It was now the summer of 1544. The
records say that the French collected at Havre
near 300 vessels, fighting ships, galleys, and transports. Doubtless the numbers are far exaggerated,
but at any rate it was the largest force ever yet
got together to invade England, capable, if well
handled, of bringing Henry to his knees. The
plan was to seize and occupy the Isle of Wight,
destroy the English fleet, then take Portsmouth
and Southampton, and so advance on London.

Henry's attention to his navy had not slackened.
He had built ship on ship. The *Great Harry*

was a thousand tons, carried 700 men, and was the
wonder of the day.   There were a dozen others
scarcely less imposing.   The King called again on
the nation, and again the nation answered.   In England altogether there were 150,000 men in arms in
field or garrison.   In the King's fleet at Portsmouth
there were 12,000 seamen, and the privateers of the
West crowded up eagerly as before.   It is strange,
with the notions which we have allowed ourselves
to form of Henry, to observe the enthusiasm with
which the whole country, as yet undivided by
doctrinal quarrels, rallied a second time to defend
him.

In this Portsmouth fleet lay undeveloped the
genius of the future naval greatness of England.
A small fact connected with it is worth recording.
The watchword on board was ' God save the King ' ;
the answer was, ' Long to reign over us ' : the
earliest germ discoverable of the English National
Anthem.

The King had come himself to Portsmouth to
witness the expected attack.   The fleet was commanded by Lord Lisle, afterwards Duke of Northumberland.   It was the middle of July.   The
French crossed from Havre unfought with, and
anchored in St. Helens Roads off Brading Harbour.
The English, being greatly inferior in numbers, lay
waiting for them inside the Spit.   The morning
after the French came in was still and sultry.   The
English could not move for want of wind.   The

galleys crossed over and engaged them for two or
three hours with some advantage. The breeze rose
at noon ; a few fast sloops got under way and
easily drove them back. But the same breeze
which enabled the English to move brought a
serious calamity with it. The *Mary Rose*, one of
Lisle's finest vessels, had been under the fire of the
galleys. Her ports had been left open, and when
the wind sprang up, she heeled over, filled, and
went down, carrying two hundred men along with
her. The French saw her sink, and thought their
own guns had done it. They hoped to follow up
their success. At night they sent over boats to
take soundings, and discover the way into the
harbour. The boats reported that the sandbanks
made the approach impossible. The French had
no clear plan of action. They tried a landing in
the island, but the force was too small, and failed.
They weighed anchor and brought up again behind
Selsea Bill, where Lisle proposed to run them
down in the dark, taking advantage of the tide.
But they had an enemy to deal with worse than
Lisle, on board their own ships, which explained
their distracted movements. Hot weather, putrid
meat, and putrid water had prostrated whole ships'
companies with dysentery. After a three weeks'
ineffectual cruise they had to hasten back to Havre,
break up, and disperse. The first great armament
which was to have recovered England to the
Papacy had effected nothing. Henry had once

more shown his strength, and was left undisputed master of the narrow seas.

So matters stood for what remained of Henry's reign. As far as he had gone, he had quarrelled with the Pope, and had brought the Church under the law. So far the country generally had gone with him, and there had been no violent changes in the administration of religion. When Henry died the Protector abolished the old creed, and created a new and perilous cleavage between Protestant and Catholic, and, while England needed the protection of a navy more than ever, allowed the fine fleet which Henry had left to fall into decay. The spirit of enterprise grew with the Reformation. Merchant companies opened trade with Russia and the Levant; adventurous sea captains went to Guinea for gold. Sir Hugh Willoughby followed the phantom of the North-west Passage, turning eastward round the North Cape to look for it, and perished in the ice. English commerce was beginning to grow in spite of the Protector's experiments ; but a new and infinitely dangerous element had been introduced by the change of religion into the relations of English sailors with the Catholic Powers, and especially with Spain. In their zeal to keep out heresy, the Spanish Government placed their harbours under the control of the Holy Office. Any vessel in which an heretical book was found was confiscated, and her crew carried to the Inquisition prisons. It had begun in Henry's time.

c

The Inquisitors attempted to treat schism as heresy
and arrest Englishmen in their ports. But Henry
spoke up stoutly to Charles V., and the Holy Office
had been made to hold its hand. All was altered
now. It was not necessary that a poor sailor
should have been found teaching heresy. It was
enough if he had an English Bible and Prayer
Book with him in his kit; and stories would come
into Dartmouth or Plymouth how some lad that
everybody knew—Bill or Jack or Tom, who had
wife or father or mother among them, perhaps—
had been seized hold of for no other crime, been
flung into a dungeon, tortured, starved, set to work
in the galleys, or burned in a fool's coat, as they
called it, at an *auto da fé* at Seville.

The object of the Inquisition was partly political : it was meant to embarrass trade and make the
people impatient of changes which produced so
much inconvenience. The effect was exactly the
opposite. Such accounts when brought home
created fury. There grew up in the seagoing
population an enthusiasm of hatred for that holy
institution, and a passionate desire for revenge.

The natural remedy would have been war; but
the division of nations was crossed by the division
of creeds ; and each nation had allies in the heart
of every other. If England went to war with Spain,
Spain could encourage insurrection among the
Catholics. If Spain or France declared war against
England, England could help the Huguenots or the

Holland Calvinists. All Governments were afraid
alike of a general war of religion which might shake
Europe in pieces. Thus individuals were left to
their natural impulses. The Holy Office burnt
English or French Protestants wherever it could
catch them. The Protestants revenged their
injuries at their own risk and in their own way,
and thus from Edward VI.'s time to the end of
the century privateering came to be the special
occupation of adventurous honourable gentlemen,
who could serve God, their country, and themselves
in fighting Catholics. Fleets of these dangerous
vessels swept the Channel, lying in wait at Scilly,
or even at the Azores—disowned in public by their
own Governments while secretly countenanced,
making war on their own account on what they
called the enemies of God. In such a business, of
course, there were many mere pirates engaged who
cared neither for God nor man. But it was the
Protestants who were specially impelled into it by
the cruelties of the Inquisition. The Holy Office
began the work with the *autos da fé*. The privateers
robbed, burnt, and scuttled Catholic ships in
retaliation. One fierce deed produced another, till
right and wrong were obscured in the passion of
religious hatred. Vivid pictures of these wild
doings survive in the English and Spanish State
Papers. Ireland was the rovers' favourite haunt.
In the universal anarchy there, a little more or a
little less did not signify. Notorious pirate cap-

tains were to be met in Cork or Kinsale, collecting
stores, casting cannon, or selling their prizes—men
of all sorts, from fanatical saints to undisguised
ruffians. Here is one incident out of many to show
the heights to which temper had risen.

'Long peace,' says someone, addressing the
Privy Council early in Elizabeth's time, ' becomes
by force of the Spanish Inquisition more hurtful
than open war. It is the secret, determined policy
of Spain to destroy the English fleet, pilots,
masters and sailors, by means of the Inquisition.
The Spanish King pretends he dares not offend the
Holy House, while we in England say we may not
proclaim war against Spain in revenge of a few.
Not long since the Spanish Inquisition executed
sixty persons of St. Malo, notwithstanding entreaty
to the King of Spain to spare them. Whereupon
the Frenchmen armed their pinnaces, lay for the
Spaniards, took a hundred and beheaded them,
sending the Spanish ships to the shore with their
heads, leaving in each ship but one man to render
the cause of the revenge. Since which time
Spanish Inquisitors have never meddled with those
of St. Malo.'

A colony of Huguenot refugees had settled on
the coast of Florida. The Spaniards heard of it,
came from St. Domingo, burnt the town, and hanged
every man, woman, and child, leaving an inscription
explaining that the poor creatures had been killed,
not as Frenchmen, but as heretics. Domenique de

Gourges, of Rochelle, heard of this fine exploit of fanaticism, equipped a ship, and sailed across. He caught the Spanish garrison which had been left in occupation and swung them on the same trees— with a second scroll saying that they were dangling there, not as Spaniards, but as murderers.

The genius of adventure tempted men of highest birth into the rovers' ranks. Sir Thomas Seymour, the Protector's brother and the King's uncle, was Lord High Admiral. In his time of office, complaints were made by foreign merchants of ships and property seized at the Thames mouth. No redress could be had ; no restitution made ; no pirate was even punished, and Seymour's personal followers were seen suspiciously decorated with Spanish ornaments. It appeared at last that Seymour had himself bought the Scilly Isles, and if he could not have his way at Court, it was said that he meant to set up there as a pirate chief.

The persecution under Mary brought in more respectable recruits than Seymour. The younger generation of the western families had grown with the times. If they were not theologically Protestant, they detested tyranny. They detested the marriage with Philip, which threatened the independence of England. At home they were powerless, but the sons of honourable houses—Strangways, Tremaynes, Staffords, Horseys, Carews, Killegrews, and Cobhams—dashed out upon the water to revenge the Smithfield massacres. They

found help where it could least have been looked
for. Henry II. of France hated heresy, but he
hated Spain worse. Sooner than see England
absorbed in the Spanish monarchy, he forgot his
bigotry in his politics. He furnished these young
mutineers with ships and money and letters of
marque. The Huguenots were their natural friends.
With Rochelle for an arsenal, they held the mouth
of the Channel, and harassed the communications
between Cadiz and Antwerp. It was a wild business : enterprise and buccaneering sanctified by
religion and hatred of cruelty ; but it was a school
like no other for seamanship, and a school for the
building of vessels which could outsail all others on
the sea ; a school, too, for the training up of hardy
men, in whose blood ran detestation of the Inquisition and the Inquisition's master. Every other
trade was swallowed up or coloured by privateering ;
the merchantmen went armed, ready for any work
that offered ; the Iceland fleet went no more in
search of cod ; the Channel boatmen forsook nets
and lines and took to livelier occupations ; Mary
was too busy burning heretics to look to the police
of the seas ; her father's fine ships rotted in harbour ; her father's coast-forts were deserted or
dismantled ; she lost Calais ; she lost the hearts of
her people in forcing them into orthodoxy ; she left
the seas to the privateers ; and no trade flourished,
save what the Catholic powers called piracy.

When Elizabeth came to the throne, the whole

merchant navy of England engaged in lawful commerce amounted to no more than 50,000 tons.
You may see more now passing every day through
the Gull Stream. In the service of the Crown
there were but seven revenue cruisers in commission, the largest 120 tons, with eight merchant
brigs altered for fighting. In harbour there were
still a score of large ships, but they were dismantled
and rotting; of artillery fit for sea work there was
none. The men were not to be had, and, as Sir
William Cecil said, to fit out ships without men was
to set armour on stakes on the sea-shore. The
mariners of England were otherwise engaged, and
in a way which did not please Cecil. He was the
ablest minister that Elizabeth had. He saw at
once that on the navy the prosperity and even the
liberty of England must eventually depend. If
England were to remain Protestant, it was not by
articles of religion or acts of uniformity that she
could be saved without a fleet at the back of them.
But he was old-fashioned. He believed in law and
order, and he has left a curious paper of reflections
on the situation. The ships' companies in Henry
VIII.'s days were recruited from the fishing smacks,
but the Reformation itself had destroyed the fishing
trade. In old times, Cecil said, no flesh was eaten
on fish days. The King himself could not have
license. Now to eat beef or mutton on fish days
was the test of a true believer. The English Iceland fishery used to supply Normandy and Brittany

as well as England. Now it had passed to the
French. The Chester men used to fish the Irish
seas. Now they had left them to the Scots. The
fishermen had taken to privateering because the
fasts of the Church were neglected. He saw it was
so. He recorded his own opinion that piracy, as
he called it, was *detestable*, and could not last. He
was to find that it could last, that it was to form
the special discipline of the generation whose business would be to fight the Spaniards. But he
struggled hard against the unwelcome conclusion.
He tried to revive lawful trade by a Navigation
Act. He tried to restore the fisheries by Act of
Parliament. He introduced a Bill recommending
godly abstinence as a means to virtue, making the
eating of meat on Fridays and Saturdays a misde-
meanour, and adding Wednesday as a half fish-day.
The House of Commons laughed at him as bringing
back Popish mummeries. To please the Protestants he inserted a clause, that the statute was
politicly meant for the increase of fishermen and
mariners, not for any superstition in the choice of
meats ; but it was no use. The Act was called in
mockery ' Cecil's Fast,' and the recovery of the
fisheries had to wait till the natural inclination of
human stomachs for fresh whiting and salt cod
should revive of itself.

Events had to take their course. Seamen were
duly provided in other ways, and such as the time
required. Privateering suited Elizabeth's con-

venience, and suited her disposition. She liked daring and adventure. She liked men who would do her work without being paid for it, men whom she could disown when expedient; who would understand her, and would not resent it. She knew her turn was to come when Philip had leisure to deal with her, if she could not secure herself meanwhile. Time was wanted to restore the navy. The privateers were a resource in the interval. They might be called pirates while there was formal peace. The name did not signify. They were really the armed force of the country. After the war broke out in the Netherlands, they had commissions from the Prince of Orange. Such commissions would not save them if taken by Spain, but it enabled them to sell their prizes, and for the rest they trusted to their speed and their guns. When Elizabeth was at war with France about Havre, she took the most noted of them into the service of the Crown. Ned Horsey became Sir Edward and Governor of the Isle of Wight; Strangways, a Red Rover in his way, who had been the terror of the Spaniards, was killed before Rouen; Tremayne fell at Havre, mourned over by Elizabeth; and Champernowne, one of the most gallant of the whole of them, was killed afterwards at Coligny's side at Moncontour.

But others took their places : the wild hawks as thick as seagulls flashing over the waves, fair wind or foul, laughing at pursuit, brave, reckless, devoted, the crews the strangest medley : English from the

Devonshire and Cornish creeks, Huguenots from
Rochelle ; Irish kernes with long skenes, ' desperate,
unruly persons with no kind of mercy.'

The Holy Office meanwhile went on in cold,
savage resolution : the Holy Office which had begun
the business and was the cause of it.

A note in Cecil's hand says that in the one year
1562 twenty-six English subjects had been burnt
at the stake in different parts of Spain.   Ten times
as many were starving in Spanish dungeons, from
which occasionally, by happy accident, a cry could
be heard like this which follows.   In 1561 an
English merchant writes from the Canaries :

' I was taken by those of the Inquisition twenty
months past, put into a little dark house two paces
long, loaded with irons, without sight of sun or
moon all that time.   When I was arraigned I was
charged that I should say our mass was as good as
theirs ; that I said I would rather give money to
the poor than buy Bulls of Rome with it.   I was
charged with being a subject to the Queen's grace,
who, they said, was enemy to the faith, Antichrist,
with other opprobrious names ; and I stood to the
defence of the Queen's Majesty, proving the infamies most untrue.   Then I was put into Little
Ease again, protesting very innocent blood to be
demanded against the judge before Christ.'

The innocent blood of these poor victims had
not to wait to be avenged at the Judgment Day.
The account was presented shortly and promptly at
the cannon's mouth.

LECTURE II

JOHN HAWKINS AND THE AFRICAN SLAVE TRADE

I BEGIN this lecture with a petition addressed to Queen Elizabeth. Thomas Seely, a merchant of Bristol, hearing a Spaniard in a Spanish port utter foul and slanderous charges against the Queen's character, knocked him down. To knock a man down for telling lies about Elizabeth might be a breach of the peace, but it had not yet been declared heresy. The Holy Office, however, seized Seely, threw him into a dungeon, and kept him starving there for three years, at the end of which he contrived to make his condition known in England. The Queen wrote herself to Philip to protest. Philip would not interfere. Seely remained in prison and in irons, and the result was a petition from his wife, in which the temper which was rising can be read as in letters of fire. Dorothy Seely demands that ' the friends of her Majesty's subjects so imprisoned and tormented in Spain may make out ships at their proper charges, take such Inquisitors or other Papistical subjects of the King of Spain as they can by sea or land,

and retain them in prison with such torments and
diet as her Majesty's subjects be kept with in
Spain, and on complaint made by the King to give
such answer as is now made when her Majesty
sues for subjects imprisoned by the Inquisition.
Or that a Commission be granted to the Archbishop
of Canterbury and the other bishops word for word
for foreign Papists as the Inquisitors have in Spain
for the Protestants. So that all may know that her
Majesty cannot and will not longer endure the
spoils and torments of her subjects, and the Spaniards shall not think this noble realm dares not
seek revenge of such importable wrongs.'

Elizabeth issued no such Commission as Dorothy
Seely asked for, but she did leave her subjects to
seek their revenge in their own way, and they
sought it sometimes too rashly.

In the summer of 1563 eight English merchantmen anchored in the roads of Gibraltar. England
and France were then at war. A French brig came
in after them, and brought up near. At sea, if
they could take her, she would have been a lawful
prize. Spaniards under similar circumstances had
not respected the neutrality of English harbours.
The Englishmen were perhaps in doubt what to
do, when the officers of the Holy Office came off to
the French ship. The sight of the black familiars
drove the English wild. Three of them made a
dash at the French ship, intending to sink her.
The Inquisitors sprang into their boat, and rowed

for their lives. The castle guns opened, and the
harbour police put out to interfere. The French ship,
however, would have been taken, when unluckily
Alvarez de Baçan, with a Spanish squadron, came
round into the Straits. Resistance was impossible.
The eight English ships were captured and carried
off to Cadiz. The English flag was trailed under
De Baçan's stern. The crews, two hundred and
forty men in all, were promptly condemned to the
galleys. In defence they could but say that the
Frenchman was an enemy, and a moderate punishment would have sufficed for a violation of the
harbour rules which the Spaniards themselves so
little regarded. But the Inquisition was inexorable, and the men were treated with such peculiar
brutality that after nine months ninety only of the
two hundred and forty were alive.

Ferocity was answered by ferocity. Listen to
this ! The Cobhams of Cowling Castle were Protestants by descent. Lord Cobham was famous in
the Lollard martyrology. Thomas Cobham, one of
the family, had taken to the sea like many of his
friends. While cruising in the Channel he caught
sight of a Spaniard on the way from Antwerp to
Cadiz with forty prisoners on board, consigned, it
might be supposed, to the Inquisition. They were,
of course, Inquisition prisoners ; for other offenders
would have been dealt with on the spot. Cobham
chased her down into the Bay of Biscay, took
her, scuttled her, and rescued the captives. But

that was not enough. The captain and crew he
sewed up in their own mainsail and flung them overboard. They were washed ashore dead, wrapped
in their extraordinary winding-sheet. Cobham was
called to account for this exploit, but he does not
seem to have been actually punished. In a very
short time he was out and away again at the
old work. There were plenty with him. After
the business at Gibraltar, Philip's subjects were
not safe in English harbours. Jacques le Clerc, a
noted privateer, called Pie de Palo from his wooden
leg, chased a Spaniard into Falmouth, and was
allowed to take her under the guns of Pendennis.
The Governor of the castle said that he could not
interfere, because Le Clerc had a commission from
the Prince of Condé. It was proved that in the
summer of 1563 there were 400 English and
Huguenot rovers in and about the Channel, and
that they had taken 700 prizes between them.
The Queen's own ships followed suit. Captain
Cotton in the *Phoenix* captured an Antwerp mer-
chantman in Flushing. The harbour-master protested. Cotton laughed, and sailed away with his
prize. The Regent Margaret wrote in indignation
to Elizabeth. Such insolence, she said, was not
to be endured. She would have Captain Cotton
chastised as an example to all others. Elizabeth
measured the situation more correctly than the
Regent ; she preferred to show Philip that she was
not afraid of him. She preferred to let her subjects

discover for themselves that the terrible Spaniard before whom the world trembled was but a colossus stuffed with clouts. Until Philip consented to tie the hands of the Holy Office she did not mean to prevent them from taking the law into their own hands.

Now and then, if occasion required, Elizabeth herself would do a little privateering on her own account. In the next story that I have to tell she appears as a principal, and her great minister, Cecil, as an accomplice. The Duke of Alva had succeeded Margaret as Regent of the Netherlands, and was drowning heresy in its own blood. The Prince of Orange was making a noble fight ; but all went ill with him. His troops were defeated, his brother Louis was killed. He was still struggling, helped by Elizabeth's money. But the odds were terrible, and the only hope lay in the discontent of Alva's soldiers, who had not been paid their wages, and would not fight without them. Philip's finances were not flourishing, but he had borrowed half a million ducats from a house at Genoa for Alva's use. The money was to be delivered in bullion at Antwerp. The Channel privateers heard that it was coming and were on the look-out for it. The vessel in which it was sent took refuge in Plymouth, but found she had run into the enemy's nest. Nineteen or twenty Huguenot and English cruisers lay round her with commissions from Condé to take every Catholic ship they met with.

Elizabeth's special friends thought and said freely that so rich a prize ought to fall to no one but her Majesty. Elizabeth thought the same, but for a more honourable reason. It was of the highest consequence that the money should not reach the Duke of Alva at that moment. Even Cecil said so, and sent the Prince of Orange word that it would be stopped in some way.

But how could it decently be done? Bishop Jewel relieved the Queen's mind (if it was ever disturbed) on the moral side of the question. The bishop held that it would be meritorious in a high degree to intercept a treasure which was to be used in the murder of Protestant Christians. But the how was the problem. To let the privateers take it openly in Plymouth harbour would, it was felt, be a scandal. Sir Arthur Champernowne, the Vice-admiral of the West, saw the difficulty and offered his services. He had three vessels of his own in Condé's privateer fleet, under his son Henry. As vice-admiral he was first in command at Plymouth. He placed a guard on board the treasure ship, telling the captain it would be a discredit to the Queen's Government if harm befell her in English waters. He then wrote to Cecil.

'If,' he said, 'it shall seem good to your honour that I with others shall give the attempt for her Majesty's use which cannot be without blood, I will not only take it in hand, but also receive the blame thereof unto myself, to the end so great a commodity.

should redound to her Grace, hoping that, after bitter storms of her displeasure, showed at the first to colour the fact, I shall find the calm of her favour in such sort as I am most willing to hazard myself to serve her Majesty. Great pity it were such a rich booty should escape her Grace. But surely I am of that mind that anything taken from that wicked nation is both necessary and profitable to our commonwealth.'

Very shocking on Sir Arthur's part to write such a letter : so many good people will think. I hope they will consider it equally shocking that King Philip should have burned English sailors at the stake because they were loyal to the laws of their own country; that he was stirring war all over Europe to please the Pope, and thrusting the doctrines of the Council of Trent down the throats of mankind at the sword's point. Spain and England might be at peace ; Romanism and Protestantism were at deadly war, and war suspends the obligations of ordinary life. Crimes the most horrible were held to be virtues in defence of the Catholic faith. The Catholics could not have the advantage of such indulgences without the inconveniences. The Protestant cause throughout Europe was one, and assailed as the Protestants were with such envenomed ferocity, they could not afford to be nicely scrupulous in the means they used to defend themselves.

Sir Arthur Champernowne was not called on to

sacrifice himself in such peculiar fashion, and a better expedient was found to secure Alva's money. The bullion was landed and was brought to London by road on the plea that the seas were unsafe. It was carried to the Tower, and when it was once inside the walls it was found to remain the property of the Genoese until it was delivered at Antwerp. The Genoese agent in London was as willing to lend it to Elizabeth as to Philip, and indeed preferred the security. Elizabeth calmly said that she had herself occasion for money, and would accept their offer. Half of it was sent to the Prince of Orange; half was spent on the Queen's navy.

Alva was of course violently angry. He arrested every English ship in the Low Countries. He arrested every Englishman that he could catch, and sequestered all English property. Elizabeth retaliated in kind. The Spanish and Flemish property taken in England proved to be worth double what had been secured by Alva. Philip could not declare war. The Netherlands insurrection was straining his resources, and with Elizabeth for an open enemy the whole weight of England would have been thrown on the side of the Prince of Orange. Elizabeth herself should have declared war, people say, instead of condescending to such tricks. Perhaps so; but also perhaps not. These insults, steadily maintained and unresented, shook the faith of mankind, and especially of her own sailors, in the invincibility of the Spanish colossus.

I am now to turn to another side of the subject. The stories which I have told you show the temper of the time, and the atmosphere which men were breathing, but it will be instructive to look more closely at individual persons, and I will take first John Hawkins (afterwards Sir John), a peculiarly characteristic figure.

The Hawkinses of Plymouth were a solid middle-class Devonshire family, who for two generations had taken a leading part in the business of the town. They still survive in the county—Achins we used to call them before school pronunciation came in, and so Philip wrote the name when the famous John began to trouble his dreams. I have already spoken of old William Hawkins, John's father, whom Henry VIII. was so fond of, and who brought over the Brazilian King. Old William had now retired and had left his place and his work to his son. John Hawkins may have been about thirty at Elizabeth's accession. He had witnessed the wild times of Edward VI. and Mary, but, though many of his friends had taken to the privateering business, Hawkins appears to have kept clear of it, and continued steadily at trade. One of these friends, and his contemporary, and in fact his near relation, was Thomas Stukely, afterwards so notorious—and a word may be said of Stukely's career as a contrast to that of Hawkins. He was a younger son of a leading county family, went to London to seek his fortune, and became a hanger-on of Sir Thomas Seymour. Doubtless he was connected with Seymour's pirating scheme at Scilly, and took to pirating as an occupation like other Western gentlemen. When Elizabeth became Queen, he introduced himself at Court and amused her with his conceit. He meant to be a king, nothing less than a king. He would go to Florida, found an empire there, and write to the Queen as his dearest sister. She gave him leave to try. He bought a vessel of 400 tons, got 100 tall soldiers to join him besides the crew, and sailed from Plymouth in 1563. Once out of harbour, he announced that the sea was to be his Florida. He went back to the pirate business, robbed freely, haunted Irish creeks, and set up an intimacy with the Ulster hero, Shan O'Neil. Shan and Stukely became bosom friends. Shan wrote to Elizabeth to recommend that she should make over Ireland to Stukely and himself to manage, and promised, if she agreed, to make it such an Ireland as had never been seen, which they probably would. Elizabeth not consenting, Stukely turned Papist, transferred his services to the Pope and Philip, and was preparing a campaign in Ireland under the Pope's direction, when he was tempted to join Sebastian of Portugal in the African expedition, and there got himself killed.

Stukely was a specimen of the foolish sort of the

young Devonshire men; Hawkins was exactly his
opposite. He stuck to business, avoided politics,
traded with Spanish ports without offending the
Holy Office, and formed intimacies and connec-
tions with the Canary Islands especially, where it
was said 'he grew much in love and favour with
the people.'

At the Canaries he naturally heard much about
the West Indies. He was adventurous. His Canaries friends told him that negroes were great mer-
chandise in the Spanish settlements in Española,
and he himself was intimately acquainted with the
Guinea coast, and knew how easily such a cargo
could be obtained.

We know to what the slave trade grew. We
have all learnt to repent of the share which England
had in it, and to abhor everyone whose hands were
stained by contact with so accursed a business.
All that may be taken for granted; but we must
look at the matter as it would have been represented at the Canaries to Hawkins himself.

The Carib races whom the Spaniards found in
Cuba and St. Domingo had withered before them
as if struck by a blight. Many died under the lash
of the Spanish overseers; many, perhaps the most,
from the mysterious causes which have made the
presence of civilisation so fatal to the Red Indian,
the Australian, and the Maori. It is with men as
it is with animals. The races which consent to be
domesticated prosper and multiply. Those which

cannot live without freedom pine like caged eagles or disappear like the buffaloes of the prairies.

Anyway, the natives perished out of the islands of the Caribbean Sea with a rapidity which startled the conquerors. The famous Bishop Las Casas pitied and tried to save the remnant that were left. The Spanish settlers required labourers for the plantations. On the continent of Africa were another race, savage in their natural state, which would domesticate like sheep and oxen, and learnt and improved in the white man's company. The negro never rose of himself out of barbarism ; as his fathers were, so he remained from age to age ; when left free, as in Liberia and in Hayti, he reverts to his original barbarism ; while in subjection to the white man he showed then, and he has shown since, high capacities of intellect and character. Such is, such was the fact. It struck Las Casas that if negroes could be introduced into the West Indian islands, the Indians might be left alone ; the negroes themselves would have a chance to rise out of their wretchedness, could be made into Christians, and could be saved at worst from the horrid fate which awaited many of them in their own country.

The black races varied like other animals : some were gentle and timid, some were ferocious as wolves. The strong tyrannised over the weak, made slaves of their prisoners, occasionally ate them, and those they did not eat they sacrificed at

what they called their *customs*—offered them up
and cut their throats at the altars of their idols.
These customs were the most sacred traditions of
the negro race. They were suspended while the
slave trade gave the prisoners a value. They
revived when the slave trade was abolished. When
Lord Wolseley a few years back entered Ashantee,
the altars were coated thick with the blood of
hundreds of miserable beings who had been freshly
slaughtered there. Still later similar horrid scenes
were reported from Dahomey. Sir Richard Burton,
who was an old acquaintance of mine, spent two
months with the King of Dahomey, and dilated to
me on the benevolence and enlightenment of that
excellent monarch. I asked why, if the King was
so benevolent, he did not alter the customs.
Burton looked at me with consternation. ' Alter
the customs ! ' he said. ' Would you have the
Archbishop of Canterbury alter the Liturgy ? '
Las Casas and those who thought as he did are not
to be charged with infamous inhumanity if they
proposed to buy these poor creatures from their
captors, save them from Mumbo Jumbo, and carry
them to countries where they would be valuable
property, and be at least as well cared for as the
mules and horses.

The experiment was tried and seemed to succeed. The negroes who were rescued from the
customs and were carried to the Spanish islands
proved docile and useful. Portuguese and Spanish

factories were established on the coast of Guinea.
The black chiefs were glad to make money out of
their wretched victims, and readily sold them.
The transport over the Atlantic became a regular
branch of business. Strict laws were made for the
good treatment of the slaves on the plantations.
The trade was carried on under license from the
Government, and an import duty of thirty ducats
per head was charged on every negro that was
landed. I call it an experiment. The full consequences could not be foreseen, and I cannot see
that as an experiment it merits the censures which
in its later developments it eventually came to
deserve. Las Casas, who approved of it, was one
of the most excellent of men. Our own Bishop
Butler could give no decided opinion against negro
slavery as it existed in his time. It is absurd to
say that ordinary merchants and ship captains
ought to have seen the infamy of a practice which
Las Casas advised and Butler could not condemn.
The Spanish and Portuguese Governments claimed,
as I said, the control of the traffic. The Spanish
settlers in the West Indies objected to a restriction
which raised the price and shortened the supply.
They considered that having established themselves
in a new country they had a right to a voice in the
conditions of their occupancy. It was thus that
the Spaniards in the Canaries represented the
matter to John Hawkins. They told him that if
he liked to make the venture with a contraband

cargo from Guinea, their countrymen would give him an enthusiastic welcome. It is evident from the story that neither he nor they expected that serious offence would be taken at Madrid. Hawkins at this time was entirely friendly with the Spaniards. It was enough if he could be assured that the colonists would be glad to deal with him.

I am not crediting him with the benevolent purposes of Las Casas. I do not suppose Hawkins thought much of saving black men's souls. He saw only an opportunity of extending his business among a people with whom he was already largely connected. The traffic was established. It had the sanction of the Church, and no objection had been raised to it anywhere on the score of morality. The only question which could have presented itself to Hawkins was of the right of the Spanish Government to prevent foreigners from getting a share of a lucrative trade against the wishes of its subjects. And his friends at the Canaries certainly did not lead him to expect any real opposition. One regrets that a famous Englishman should have been connected with the slave trade ; but we have no right to heap violent censures upon him because he was no more enlightened than the wisest of his contemporaries.

Thus, encouraged from Santa Cruz, Hawkins on his return to England formed an African company out of the leading citizens of London. Three vessels were fitted out, Hawkins being commander

and part owner. The size of them is remarkable :
the *Solomon*, as the largest was called, 120 tons ;
the *Swallow*, 100 tons ; the *Jonas* not above 40 tons.
This represents them as inconceivably small. They
carried between them a hundred men, and ample
room had to be provided besides for the blacks.
There may have been a difference in the measurement of tonnage. We ourselves have five stan-
dards : builder's measurement, yacht measurement,
displacement, sail area, and register measurement.
Registered tonnage is far under the others : a yacht
registered 120 tons would be called 200 in a shipping list. However that be, the brigantines and
sloops used by the Elizabethans on all adventurous
expeditions were mere boats compared with what
we should use now on such occasions. The reason
was obvious. Success depended on speed and
sailing power. The art of building big square-
rigged ships which would work to windward had
not been yet discovered, even by Mr. Fletcher of
Rye. The fore-and-aft rig alone would enable a
vessel to tack, as it is called, and this could only be
used with craft of moderate tonnage.

The expedition sailed in October 1562. They
called at the Canaries, where they were warmly
entertained. They went on to Sierra Leone, where
they collected 300 negroes. They avoided the
Government factories, and picked them up as they
could, some by force, some by negotiation with
local chiefs, who were as ready to sell their subjects

as Sancho Panza intended to be when he got his island. They crossed without misadventure to St. Domingo, where Hawkins represented that he was on a voyage of discovery ; that he had been driven out of his course and wanted food and money. He said he had certain slaves with him, which he asked permission to sell. What he had heard at the Canaries turned out to be exactly true. So far as the Governor of St. Domingo knew, Spain and England were at peace. Privateers had not troubled the peace of the Caribbean Sea, or dangerous heretics menaced the Catholic faith there. Inquisitors might have been suspicious, but the Inquisition had not yet been established beyond the Atlantic. The Queen of England was his sovereign's sister-in-law, and the Governor saw no reason why he should construe his general instructions too literally. The planters were eager to buy, and he did not wish to be unpopular. He allowed Hawkins to sell two out of his three hundred negroes, leaving the remaining hundred as a deposit should question be raised about the duty. Evidently the only doubt in the Governor's mind was whether the Madrid authorities would charge foreign importers on a higher scale. The question was new. No stranger had as yet attempted to trade there.

Everyone was satisfied, except the negroes, who were not asked their opinion. The profits were enormous. A ship in the harbour was about to sail for Cadiz. Hawkins invested most of what he had made in a cargo of hides, for which, as he understood, there was a demand in Spain, and he sent them over in her in charge of one of his partners. The Governor gave him a testimonial for good conduct during his stay in the port, and with this and with his three vessels he returned leisurely to England, having, as he imagined, been splendidly successful.

He was to be unpleasantly undeceived. A few days after he had arrived at Plymouth, he met the man whom he had sent to Cadiz with the hides forlorn and empty-handed. The Inquisition, he said, had seized the cargo and confiscated it. An order had been sent to St. Domingo to forfeit the reserved slaves. He himself had escaped for his life, as the familiars had been after him.

Nothing shows more clearly how little thought there had been in Hawkins that his voyage would have given offence in Spain than the astonishment with which he heard the news. He protested. He wrote to Philip. Finding entreaties useless, he swore vengeance ; but threats were equally ineffectual. Not a hide, not a farthing could he recover. The Spanish Government, terrified at the intrusion of English adventurers into their western paradise to endanger the gold fleets, or worse to endanger the purity of the faith, issued orders more peremptory than ever to close the ports there against all foreigners. Philip personally warned Sir Thomas Chaloner, the English ambassador, that if such visits were repeated, mischief would come of it. And Cecil, who disliked all such semi-piratical enterprises, and Chaloner, who was half a Spaniard and an old companion in arms of Charles V., entreated their mistress to forbid them.

Elizabeth, however, had her own views in such matters. She liked money. She liked encouraging the adventurous disposition of her subjects, who were fighting the State's battles at their own risk and cost. She saw in Philip's anger a confession that the West Indies was his vulnerable point ; and that if she wished to frighten him into letting her alone, and to keep the Inquisition from burning her sailors, there was the place where Philip would be more sensitive. Probably, too, she thought that Hawkins had done nothing for which he could be justly blamed. He had traded at St. Domingo with the Governor's consent, and confiscation was sharp practice.

This was clearly Hawkins's own view of the matter. He had injured no one. He had offended no pious ears by parading his Protestantism. He was not Philip's subject, and was not to be expected to know the instructions given by the Spanish Government in the remote corners of their dominions. If anyone was to be punished, it was not he but the Governor. He held that he had been robbed, and had a right to indemnify himself at the King's expense. He would go out again. He was certain of a cordial reception from the planters. Between him and them there was the friendliest understanding. His quarrel was with Philip, and Philip only. He meant to sell a fresh cargo of negroes, and the Madrid Government should go without their 30 per cent. duty.

Elizabeth approved. Hawkins had opened the road to the West Indies. He had shown how easy slave smuggling was, and how profitable it was; how it was also possible for the English to establish friendly relations with the Spanish settlers in the West Indies, whether Philip liked it or not. Another company was formed for a second trial. Elizabeth took shares, Lord Pembroke took shares, and other members of the Council. The Queen lent the *Jesus*, a large ship of her own, of 700 tons. Formal instructions were given that no wrong was to be done to the King of Spain, but what wrong might mean was left to the discretion of the commander. Where the planters were all eager to purchase, means of traffic would be discovered without collision with the authorities. This time the expedition was to be on a larger scale, and a hundred soldiers were put on board to provide for contingencies. Thus furnished, Hawkins started on his second voyage in October 1564. The autumn was chosen, to avoid the extreme tropical heats. He touched as before to see his friends at the Canaries. He went on to the Rio Grande, met with adventures bad and good, found a chief at war with a neighbouring tribe, helped to capture a town and take prisoners, made purchases at a Portuguese factory. In this way he now secured 400 human cattle, perhaps for a better fate than they would have met with at home, and with these he sailed off in the old direction. Near the equator he fell in with calms ; he was short of water, and feared to lose some of them ; but, as the record of the voyage puts it, ' Almighty God would not suffer His elect to perish,' and sent a breeze which carried him safe to Dominica. In that wettest of islands he found water in plenty, and had then to consider what next he would do. St. Domingo, he thought, would be no longer safe for him ; so he struck across to the Spanish Main to a place called Burboroata, where he might hope that nothing would be known about him. In this he was mistaken. Philip's orders had arrived : no Englishman of any creed or kind was to be allowed to trade in his West India dominions. The settlers, however, intended to trade. They required only a display of force that they might pretend that they were yielding to compulsion. Hawkins told his old story. He said that he was out on the service of the Queen of England. He had been driven off his course by bad weather. He was short of supplies and had many men on board, who might do the town some mischief if they were not allowed to land peaceably and buy and sell what they wanted. The Governor affecting to hesitate, he threw 120 men on shore, and brought his guns to bear

on the castle. The Governor gave way under protest. Hawkins was to be permitted to sell half his
negroes. He said that as he had been treated so
inhospitably he would not pay the 30 per cent.
The King of Spain should have 7½, and no more.
The settlers had no objection. The price would be
the less, and with this deduction his business was
easily finished off. He bought no more hides, and
was paid in solid silver.

From Burboroata he went on to Rio de la Hacha,
where the same scene was repeated. The whole
400 were disposed of, this time with ease and
complete success. He had been rapid, and had
the season still before him. Having finished his
business, he surveyed a large part of the Caribbean
Sea, taking soundings, noting the currents, and
making charts of the coasts and islands. This
done, he turned homewards, following the east
shore of North America as far as Newfoundland.
There he gave his crew a change of diet, with fresh
cod from the Banks, and after eleven months'
absence he sailed into Padstow, having lost but
twenty men in the whole adventure, and bringing
back 60 per cent. to the Queen and the other
shareholders.

Nothing succeeds like success. Hawkins's
praises were in everyone's mouth, and in London
he was the hero of the hour. Elizabeth received
him at the palace. The Spanish ambassador, De
Silva, met him there at dinner. He talked freely

of where he had been and of what he had done,
only keeping back the gentle violence which he
had used. He regarded this as a mere farce, since
there had been no one hurt on either side. He
boasted of having given the greatest satisfaction to
the Spaniards who had dealt with him. De Silva
could but bow, report to his master, and ask instructions how he was to proceed.

Philip was frightfully disturbed. He saw in
prospect his western subjects allying themselves
with the English—heresy creeping in among them ;
his gold fleets in danger, all the possibilities with
which Elizabeth had wished to alarm him. He
read and re-read De Silva's letters, and opposite
the name of Achines he wrote startled interjections
on the margin : ' Ojo! Ojo ! '

The political horizon was just then favourable
to Elizabeth. The Queen of Scots was a prisoner
in Loch Leven ; the Netherlands were in revolt ;
the Huguenots were looking up in France ; and
when Hawkins proposed a third expedition, she
thought that she could safely allow it. She gave him
the use of the *Jesus* again, with another smaller
ship of hers, the *Minion*. He had two of his own
still fit for work ; and a fifth, the *Judith*, was
brought in by his young cousin, Francis Drake, who
was now to make his first appearance on the stage.
I shall tell you by-and-by who and what Drake
was. Enough to say now that he was a relation of
Hawkins, the owner of a small smart sloop or

E

brigantine, and ambitious of a share in a stirring
business.

The Plymouth seamen were falling into dangerous contempt of Philip. While the expedition
was fitting out, a ship of the King's came into Cat-
water with more prisoners from Flanders. She
was flying the Castilian flag, contrary to rule, it
was said, in English harbours. The treatment of
the English ensign at Gibraltar had not been for-
given, and Hawkins ordered the Spanish captain
to strike his colours. The captain refused, and
Hawkins instantly fired into him. In the confusion
the prisoners escaped on board the *Jesus* and were
let go. The captain sent a complaint to London,
and Cecil—who disapproved of Hawkins and all
his proceedings—sent down an officer to inquire
into what had happened. Hawkins, confident in
Elizabeth's protection, quietly answered that the
Spaniard had broken the laws of the port, and
that it was necessary to assert the Queen's
authority.

' Your mariners,' said De Silva to her, ' rob our
subjects on the sea, trade where they are forbidden
to go, and fire upon our ships in your harbours.
Your preachers insult my master from their pulpits,
and when we remonstrate we are answered with
menaces. We have borne so far with their injuries,
attributing them rather to temper and bad manners
than to deliberate purpose. But, seeing that no
redress can be had, and that the same treatment

of us continues, I must consult my Sovereign's
pleasure. For the last time, I require your Majesty
to punish this outrage at Plymouth and preserve
the peace between the two realms.'

No remonstrance could seem more just till the
other side was heard. The other side was that the
Pope and the Catholic powers were undertaking to
force the Protestants of France and Flanders back
under the Papacy with fire and sword. It was no
secret that England's turn was to follow as soon as
Philip's hands were free. Meanwhile he had been
intriguing with the Queen of Scots ; he had been
encouraging Ireland in rebellion ; he had been per-
secuting English merchants and seamen, starving
them to death in the Inquisition dungeons, or burning them at the stake. The Smithfield infamies
were fresh in Protestant memories, and who could
tell how soon the horrid work would begin again
at home, if the Catholic powers could have their
way ?

If the King of Spain and his Holiness at Rome
would have allowed other nations to think and
make laws for themselves, pirates and privateers
would have disappeared off the ocean. The West
Indies would have been left undisturbed, and
Spanish, English, French, and Flemings would
have lived peacefully side by side as they do now.
But spiritual tyranny had not yet learned its lesson,
and the ' Beggars of the Sea ' were to be Philip's
schoolmasters in irregular but effective fashion.

Elizabeth listened politely to what De Silva said, promised to examine into his complaints, and allowed Hawkins to sail.

What befell him you will hear in the next lecture.

LECTURE III

SIR JOHN HAWKINS AND PHILIP THE SECOND

My last lecture left Hawkins preparing to start on his third and, as it proved, most eventful voyage. I mentioned that he was joined by a young relation, of whom I must say a few preliminary words. Francis Drake was a Devonshire man, like Hawkins himself and Raleigh and Davis and Gilbert, and many other famous men of those days. He was born at Tavistock somewhere about 1540. He told Camden that he was of mean extraction. He meant merely that he was proud of his parents and made no idle pretensions to noble birth. His father was a tenant of the Earl of Bedford, and must have stood well with him, for Francis Russell, the heir of the earldom, was the boy's godfather. From him Drake took his Christian name. The Drakes were early converts to Protestantism. Trouble rising at Tavistock on the Six Articles Bill, they removed to Kent, where the father, probably through Lord Bedford's influence, was appointed a lay chaplain in Henry VIII.'s fleet at Chatham. In the next reign, when the Protestants were upper-most, he was ordained and became vicar of Upnor

on the Medway. Young Francis took early to the
water, and made acquaintance with a ship-master
trading to the Channel ports, who took him on
board his ship and bred him as a sailor. The boy
distinguished himself, and his patron when he died
left Drake his vessel in his will. For several years
Drake stuck steadily to his coasting work, made
money, and made a solid reputation. His ambition
grew with his success. The seagoing English were
all full of Hawkins and his West Indian exploits.
The Hawkinses and the Drakes were near relations.
Hearing that there was to be another expedition,
and having obtained his cousin's consent, Francis
Drake sold his brig, bought the *Judith*, a handier
and faster vessel, and with a few stout sailors from
the river went down to Plymouth and joined.

De Silva had sent word to Philip that Hawkins
was again going out, and preparations had been
made to receive him. Suspecting nothing, Hawkins
with his four consorts sailed, as before, in October
1567. The start was ominous. He was caught
and badly knocked about by an equinoctial in the
Bay of Biscay. He lost his boats. The *Jesus*
strained her timbers and leaked, and he so little
liked the look of things that he even thought of
turning back and giving up the expedition for the
season. However, the weather mended. They put
themselves to rights at the Canaries, picked up
their spirits, and proceeded. The slave-catching
was managed successfully, though with some

increased difficulty. The cargo with equal success
was disposed of at the Spanish settlements. At
one place the planters came off in their boats at
night to buy. At Rio de la Hacha, where the most
imperative orders had been sent to forbid his
admittance, Hawkins landed a force as before and
took possession of the town, of course with the
connivance of the settlers. At Carthagena he was
similarly ordered off, and as Carthagena was
strongly fortified he did not venture to meddle with
it. But elsewhere he found ample markets for his
wares. He sold all his blacks. By this and by
other dealings he had collected what is described
as a vast treasure of gold, silver, and jewels. The
hurricane season was approaching, and he made the
best of his way homewards with his spoils, in the
fear of being overtaken by it. Unluckily for him,
he had lingered too long. He had passed the west
point of Cuba and was working up the back of the
island when a hurricane came down on him. The
gale lasted four days. The ships' bottoms were
foul and they could make no way. Spars were lost
and rigging carried away. The *Jesus*, which had
not been seaworthy all along, leaked worse than
ever and lost her rudder. Hawkins looked for some
port in Florida, but found the coast shallow and
dangerous, and was at last obliged to run for
San Juan de Ulloa, at the bottom of the Gulf of
Mexico.

San Juan de Ulloa is a few miles only from

Vera Cruz. It was at that time the chief port of Mexico, through which all the traffic passed between the colony and the mother-country, and was thus a place of some consequence. It stands on a small bay facing towards the north. Across the mouth of this bay lies a narrow ridge of sand and shingle, half a mile long, which acts as a natural breakwater and forms the harbour. This ridge, or island as it was called, was uninhabited, but it had been faced on the inner front by a wall. The water was deep alongside, and vessels could thus lie in perfect security, secured by their cables to rings let into the masonry.

The prevailing wind was from the north, bringing in a heavy surf on the back of the island. There was an opening at both ends, but only one available for vessels of large draught. In this the channel was narrow, and a battery at the end of the breakwater would completely command it. The town stood on the opposite side of the bay.

Into a Spanish port thus constructed Hawkins entered with his battered squadron on September 16, 1568. He could not have felt entirely easy. But he probably thought that he had no ill-will to fear from the inhabitants generally, and that the Spanish authorities would not be strong enough to meddle with him. His ill star had brought him there at a time when Alvarez de Baçan, the same officer who had destroyed the English ships at Gibraltar, was daily expected from Spain—sent by Philip, as it proved, specially to look for him. Hawkins, when he appeared outside, had been mistaken for the Spanish admiral, and it was under this impression that he had been allowed to enter. The error was quickly discovered on both sides.

Though still ignorant that he was himself De Baçan's particular object, yet De Baçan was the last officer whom in his crippled condition he would have cared to encounter. Several Spanish merchantmen were in the port richly loaded: with these of course he did not meddle, though, if reinforced, they might perhaps meddle with him. As his best resource he despatched a courier on the instant to Mexico to inform the Viceroy of his arrival, to say that he had an English squadron with him; that he had been driven in by stress of weather and need of repairs; that the Queen was an ally of the King of Spain; and that, as he understood a Spanish fleet was likely soon to arrive, he begged the Viceroy to make arrangements to prevent disputes.

As yet, as I said in the last lecture, there was no Inquisition in Mexico. It was established there three years later, for the special benefit of the English. But so far there was no ill-will towards the English—rather the contrary. Hawkins had hurt no one, and the negro trading had been eminently popular. The Viceroy might perhaps have connived at Hawkins's escape, but again by ill-fortune he was himself under orders of recall, and his successor was coming out in this particular fleet with De Baçan.

Had he been well disposed and free to act it would still have been too late, for the very next morning, September 17, De Baçan was off the harbour mouth with thirteen heavily armed galleons and frigates. The smallest of them carried probably 200 men, and the odds were now tremendous. Hawkins's vessels lay ranged along the inner bank or wall of the island. He instantly occupied the island itself and mounted guns at the point covering the way in. He then sent a boat off to De Baçan to say that he was an Englishman, that he was in possession of the port, and must forbid the entrance of the Spanish fleet till he was assured that there was to be no violence. It was a strong measure to shut a Spanish admiral out of a Spanish port in a time of profound peace. Still, the way in was difficult, and could not be easily forced if resolutely defended. The northerly wind was rising; if it blew into a gale the Spaniards would be on a lee shore. Under desperate circumstances, desperate things will be done. Hawkins in his subsequent report thus explains his dilemma :—

'I was in two difficulties. Either I must keep them out of the port, which with God's grace I could easily have done, in which case with a northerly wind rising they would have been wrecked, and I should have been answerable; or I

must risk their playing false, which on the whole
I preferred to do.'

The northerly gale it appears did not rise, or
the English commander might have preferred the
first alternative. Three days passed in negotiation.
De Baçan and Don Enriquez, the new Viceroy, were
naturally anxious to get into shelter out of a
dangerous position, and were equally desirous not
to promise any more than was absolutely necessary.
The final agreement was that De Baçan and the
fleet should enter without opposition. Hawkins
might stay till he had repaired his damages, and
buy and sell what he wanted; and further, as long
as they remained the English were to keep
possession of the island. This article, Hawkins
says, was long resisted, but was consented to at
last. It was absolutely necessary, for with the
island in their hands, the Spaniards had only to
cut the English cables, and they would have driven
ashore across the harbour.

The treaty so drawn was formally signed.
Hostages were given on both sides, and De Baçan
came in. The two fleets were moored as far apart
from each other as the size of the port would allow.
Courtesies were exchanged, and for two days all
went well. It is likely that the Viceroy and the admiral did not at first know that it was the very man
whom they had been sent out to sink or capture
who was lying so close to them. When they did
know it they may have looked on him as a pirate,

with whom, as with heretics, there was no need to
keep faith. Any way, the rat was in the trap, and
De Baçan did not mean to let him out. The
Jesus lay furthest in; the *Minion* lay beyond
her towards the entrance, moored apparently to a
ring on the quay, but free to move; and the
Judith, further out again, moored in the same
way. Nothing is said of the two small vessels
remaining.

De Baçan made his preparations silently,
covered by the town. He had men in abundance
ready to act where he should direct. On the third
day, the 20th of September, at noon, the *Minion's*
crew had gone to dinner, when they saw a large hulk
of 900 tons slowly towing up alongside of them. Not
liking such a neighbour, they had their cable ready
to slip and began to set their canvas. On a sudden
shots and cries were heard from the town. Parties
of English who were on land were set upon; many
were killed; the rest were seen flinging themselves
into the water and swimming off to the ships. At
the same instant the guns of the galleons and of
the shore batteries opened fire on the *Jesus* and
her consorts, and in the smoke and confusion
300 Spaniards swarmed out of the hulk and
sprang on the *Minion's* decks. The *Minion's*
men instantly cut them down or drove them overboard, hoisted sail, and forced their way out of
the harbour, followed by the *Judith*. The *Jesus*
was left alone, unable to stir. She defended her-

self desperately. In the many actions which were fought afterwards between the English and the Spaniards, there was never any more gallant or more severe. De Baçan's own ship was sunk and the vice-admiral's was set on fire. The Spanish, having an enormous advantage in numbers, were able to land a force on the island, seize the English battery there, cut down the gunners, and turn the guns close at hand on the devoted *Jesus*. Still she fought on, defeating every attempt to board, till at length De Baçan sent down fire-ships on her, and then the end came. All that Hawkins had made by his voyage, money, bullion, the ship herself, had to be left to their fate. Hawkins himself with the survivors of the crew took to their boats, dashed through the enemy, who vainly tried to take them, and struggled out after the *Minion* and the *Judith*. It speaks ill for De Baçan that with so large a force at his command, and in such a position, a single Englishman escaped to tell the story.

Even when outside Hawkins's situation was still critical and might well be called desperate. The *Judith* was but fifty tons ; the *Minion* not above a hundred. They were now crowded up with men. They had little water on board, and there had been no time to refill their store-chests, or fit themselves for sea. Happily the weather was moderate. If the wind had risen, nothing could have saved them. They anchored two miles off to put themselves in some sort of order. The Spanish fleet did not venture to molest further so desperate a foe. On Saturday the 25th they set sail, scarcely knowing whither to turn. To attempt an ocean voyage as they were would be certain destruction, yet they could not trust longer to De Baçan's cowardice or forbearance. There was supposed to be a shelter of some kind somewhere on the east side of the Gulf of Mexico, where it was hoped they might obtain provisions. They reached the place on October 8, but found nothing. English sailors have never been wanting in resolution. They knew that if they all remained on board every one of them must starve. A hundred volunteered to land and take their chance. The rest on short rations might hope to make their way home. The sacrifice was accepted. The hundred men were put on shore. They wandered for a few days in the woods, feeding on roots and berries, and shot at by the Indians. At length they reached a Spanish station, where they were taken and sent as prisoners to Mexico. There was, as I said, no Holy Office as yet in Mexico. The new Viceroy, though he had been in the fight at San Juan de Ulloa, was not implacable. They were treated at first with humanity ; they were fed, clothed, taken care of, and then distributed among the plantations. Some were employed as overseers, some as mechanics. Others, who understood any kind of business, were allowed to settle in towns, make money, and even marry and establish themselves.

Perhaps Philip heard of it, and was afraid that so many heretics might introduce the plague. The quiet time lasted three years ; at the end of those years the Inquisitors arrived, and then, as if these poor men had been the special object of that delightful institution, they were hunted up, thrown into dungeons, examined on their faith, tortured, some burnt in an *auto da fé*, some lashed through the streets of Mexico naked on horseback and returned to their prisons. Those who did not die under this pious treatment were passed over to the Holy Office at Seville and were condemned to the galleys.

Here I leave them for the moment. We shall presently hear of them again in a very singular connection. The *Minion* and *Judith* meanwhile pursued their melancholy way. They parted company. The *Judith*, being the better sailer, arrived first, and reached Plymouth in December, torn and tattered. Drake rode off post immediately to carry the bad news to London. The *Minion's* fate was worse. She made her course through the Bahama Channel, her crew dying as if struck with a pestilence, till at last there were hardly men enough left to handle the sails. They fell too far south for England, and at length had to put into Vigo, where their probable fate would be a Spanish prison. Happily they found other English vessels in the roads there. Fresh hands were put on board, and fresh provisions. With these supplies Hawkins reached Mount's Bay a month later than the *Judith*, in January 1569.

Drake had told the story, and all England was ringing with it. Englishmen always think their own countrymen are in the right. The Spaniards, already in evil odour with the sea-going population, were accused of abominable treachery. The splendid fight which Hawkins had made raised him into a national idol, and though he had suffered financially, his loss was made up in reputation and authority. Every privateer in the West was eager to serve under the leadership of the hero of San Juan de Ulloa. He speedily found himself in command of a large irregular squadron, and even Cecil recognised his consequence. His chief and constant anxiety was for the comrades whom he had left behind, and he talked of a new expedition to recover them, or revenge them if they had been killed ; but all things had to wait. They probably found means of communicating with him, and as long as there was no Inquisition in Mexico, he may have learnt that there was no immediate occasion for action.

Elizabeth put a brave face on her disappointment. She knew that she was surrounded with treason, but she knew also that the boldest course was the safest. She had taken Alva's money, and was less than ever inclined to restore it. She had the best of the bargain in the arrest of the Spanish and English ships and cargoes. Alva would not encourage Philip to declare war with England till the Netherlands were completely reduced, and Philip, with his leaden foot (*pié de plomo*), always preferred patience and intrigue. Time and he and the Pope were three powers which in the end, he thought, would prove irresistible, and indeed it seemed, after Hawkins's return, as if Philip would turn out to be right. The presence of the Queen of Scots in England had set in flame the Catholic nobles. The wages of Alva's troops had been wrung somehow out of the wretched Provinces, and his supreme ability and inexorable resolution were steadily grinding down the revolt. Every port in Holland and Zealand was in Alva's hands. Elizabeth's throne was undermined by the Ridolfi conspiracy, the most dangerous which she had ever had to encounter. The only Protestant fighting power left on the sea which could be entirely depended on was in the privateer fleet, sailing, most of them, under a commission from the Prince of Orange.

This fleet was the strangest phenomenon in naval history. It was half Dutch, half English, with a flavour of Huguenot, and was commanded by a Flemish noble, Count de la Mark. Its headquarters were in the Downs or Dover Roads, where it could watch the narrow seas, and seize every Spanish ship that passed which was not too strong to be meddled with. The cargoes taken were openly sold in Dover market. If the Spanish ambassador is to be believed in a complaint which

F

he addressed to Cecil, Spanish gentlemen taken
prisoners were set up to public auction there for
the ransom which they would fetch, and were disposed of for one hundred pounds each. If Alva
sent cruisers from Antwerp to burn them out, they
retreated under the guns of Dover Castle. Roving
squadrons of them flew down to the Spanish coasts,
pillaged churches, carried off church plate, and the
captains drank success to piracy at their banquets
out of chalices. The Spanish merchants at last
estimated the property destroyed at three million ducats, and they said that if their flag could
no longer protect them, they must decline to make
further contracts for the supply of the Netherlands
army.

It was life or death to Elizabeth. The Ridolfi
plot, an elaborate and far-reaching conspiracy to
give her crown to Mary Stuart and to make away
with heresy, was all but complete. The Pope and
Philip had approved; Alva was to invade; the
Duke of Norfolk was to head an insurrection in the
Eastern Counties. Never had she been in greater
danger. Elizabeth was herself to be murdered.
The intention was known, but the particulars of
the conspiracy had been kept so secret that she had
not evidence enough to take measures to protect
herself. The privateers at Dover were a sort of
protection; they would at least make Alva's crossing
more difficult; but the most pressing exigency was
the discovery of the details of the treason. Nothing

was to be gained by concession; the only salvation
was in daring.

At Antwerp there was a certain Doctor Story,
maintained by Alva there to keep a watch on
English heretics. Story had been a persecutor
under Mary, and had defended heretic burning in
Elizabeth's first Parliament. He had refused the
oath of allegiance, had left the country, and had
taken to treason. Cecil wanted evidence, and this
man he knew could give it. A pretended informer
brought Story word that there was an English
vessel in the Scheldt which he would find worth
examining. Story was tempted on board. The
hatches were closed over him. He was delivered
two days after at the Tower, when his secrets were
squeezed out of him by the rack and he was then
hanged.

Something was learnt, but less still than Cecil
needed to take measures to protect the Queen. And
now once more, and in a new character, we are to
meet John Hawkins. Three years had passed since
the catastrophe at San Juan de Ulloa. He had
learnt to his sorrow that his poor companions had
fallen into the hands of the Holy Office at last; had
been burnt, lashed, starved in dungeons or worked
in chains in the Seville yards; and his heart, not
a very tender one, bled at the thoughts of them.
The finest feature in the seamen of those days was
their devotion to one another. Hawkins determined
that, one way or other, these old comrades of his

should be rescued. Entreaties were useless ; force was impossible. There might still be a chance with cunning. He would risk anything, even the loss of his soul, to save them.

De Silva had left England. The Spanish ambassador was now Don Guerau or Gerald de Espes, and to him had fallen the task of watching and directing the conspiracy. Philip was to give the signal, the Duke of Norfolk and other Catholic peers were to rise and proclaim the Queen of Scots. Success would depend on the extent of the disaffection in England itself ; and the ambassador's business was to welcome and encourage all symptoms of discontent. Hawkins knew generally what was going on, and he saw in it an opportunity of approaching Philip on his weak side. Having been so much in the Canaries, he probably spoke Spanish fluently. He called on Don Guerau, and with audacious coolness represented that he and many of his friends were dissatisfied with the Queen's service. He said he had found her faithless and ungrateful, and he and they would gladly transfer their allegiance to the King of Spain, if the King of Spain would receive them. For himself, he would undertake to bring over the whole privateer fleet of the West, and in return he asked for nothing but the release of a few poor English seamen who were in prison at Seville.

Don Guerau was full of the belief that the whole nation was ready to rebel. He eagerly swallowed the bait which Hawkins threw to him. He wrote to Alva, he wrote to Philip's secretary, Cayas, expatiating on the importance of securing such an addition to their party. It was true, he admitted, that Hawkins had been a pirate, but piracy was a common fault of the English, and no wonder when the Spaniards submitted to being plundered so meekly; the man who was offering his services was bold, resolute, capable, and had great influence with the English sailors; he strongly advised that such a recruit should be encouraged.

Alva would not listen. Philip, who shuddered at the very name of Hawkins, was incredulous. Don Guerau had to tell Sir John that the King at present declined his offer, but advised him to go himself to Madrid, or to send some confidential friend with assurances and explanations.

Another figure now enters on the scene, a George Fitzwilliam. I do not know who he was, or why Hawkins chose him for his purpose. The Duke of Feria was one of Philip's most trusted ministers. He had married an English lady who had been a maid of honour to Queen Mary. It is possible that Fitzwilliam had some acquaintance with her or with her family. At any rate, he went to the Spanish Court; he addressed himself to the Ferias; he won their confidence, and by their means was admitted to an interview with Philip. He represented Hawkins as a faithful Catholic who was indignant at the progress of heresy in England,

who was eager to assist in the overthrow of Elizabeth and the elevation of the Queen of Scots,
and was able and willing to carry along with him
the great Western privateer fleet, which had become
so dreadful to the Spanish mind. Philip listened
and was interested. It was only natural, he thought,
that heretics should be robbers and pirates. If they
could be recovered to the Church, their bad habits
would leave them. The English navy was the
most serious obstacle to the intended invasion.
Still, Hawkins! The Achines of his nightmares!
It could not be. He asked Fitzwilliam if his friend
was acquainted with the Queen of Scots or the Duke
of Norfolk. Fitzwilliam was obliged to say that he
was not. The credentials of John Hawkins were
his own right hand. He was making the King a
magnificent offer : nothing less than a squadron of
the finest ships in the world—not perhaps in the
best condition, he added, with cool British
impudence, owing to the Queen's parsimony, but
easily to be put in order again if the King would
pay the seamen's wages and advance some money
for repairs. The release of a few poor prisoners
was a small price to ask for such a service.

The King was still wary, watching the bait like
an old pike, but hesitating to seize it ; but the duke
and duchess were willing to be themselves securities
for Fitzwilliam's faith, and Philip promised at last
that if Hawkins would send him a letter of re-
commendation from the Queen of Scots herself, he

would then see what could be done. The Ferias
were dangerously enthusiastic. They talked freely
to Fitzwilliam of the Queen of Scots and her
prospects. They trusted him with letters and
presents to her which would secure his admittance
to her confidence. Hawkins had sent him over for
the single purpose of cheating Philip into releasing
his comrades from the Inquisition ; and he had been
introduced to secrets of high political moment ; like
Saul, the son of Kish, he had gone to seek his
father's asses and he had found a kingdom. Fitzwilliam hurried home with his letters and his news.
Things were now serious. Hawkins could act no
further on his own responsibility. He consulted
Cecil. Cecil consulted the Queen, and it was agreed
that the practice, as it was called, should be carried
further. It might lead to the discovery of the
whole secret.

Very treacherous, think some good people.
Well, there are times when one admires even
treachery—

nec lex est justior ulla
Quam necis artifices arte perire sua.

King Philip was confessedly preparing to encourage
an English subject in treason to his sovereign.
Was it so wrong to hoist the engineer with his own
petard ? Was it wrong of Hamlet to finger the
packet of Rosencrantz and Guildenstern and rewrite
his uncle's despatch ? Let us have done with cant
in these matters. Mary Stuart was at Sheffield

Castle in charge of Lord Shrewsbury, and Fitz-william could not see her without an order from the Crown. Shrewsbury, though loyal to Elizabeth, was notoriously well inclined to Mary, and there-fore could not be taken into confidence. In writing to him Cecil merely said that friends of Fitz-william's were in prison in Spain ; that if the Queen of Scots would intercede for them, Philip might be induced to let them go. He might therefore allow Fitzwilliam to have a private audience with that Queen.

Thus armed, Fitzwilliam went down to Sheffield. He was introduced. He began with presenting Mary with the letters and remembrances from the Ferias, which at once opened her heart. It was impossible for her to suspect a friend of the duke and duchess. She was delighted at receiving a visitor from the Court of Spain. She was prudent enough to avoid dangerous confidences, but she said she was always pleased when she could do a service to Englishmen, and with all her heart would intercede for the prisoners. She wrote to Philip, she wrote to the duke and duchess, and gave the letters to Fitzwilliam to deliver. He took them to London, called on Don Gerald, and told him of his success. Don Gerald also wrote to his master, wrote unguardedly, and also trusted Fitzwilliam with the despatch.

The various packets were taken first to Cecil, and were next shown to the Queen. They were then returned to Fitzwilliam, who once more went off with them to Madrid. If the letters produced the expected effect, Cecil calmly observed that divers commodities would ensue. English sailors would be released from the Inquisition and the galleys. The enemy's intentions would be discovered. If the King of Spain could be induced to do as Fitzwilliam had suggested, and assist in the repairs of the ships at Plymouth, credit would be obtained for a sum of money which could be employed to his own detriment. If Alva attempted the projected invasion, Hawkins might take the ships as if to escort him, and then do some notable exploit in mid-Channel.

You will observe the downright directness of Cecil, Hawkins, and the other parties in the matter. There is no wrapping up their intentions in fine phrases, no parade of justification. They went straight to their point. It was very characteristic of Englishmen in those stern, dangerous times. They looked facts in the face, and did what fact required. All really happened exactly as I have described it : the story is told in letters and documents of the authenticity of which there is not the smallest doubt.

We will follow Fitzwilliam. He arrived at the Spanish Court at the moment when Ridolfi had brought from Rome the Pope's blessing on the conspiracy. The final touches were being added by the Spanish Council of State. All was hope ;

all was the credulity of enthusiasm! Mary Stuart's
letter satisfied Philip. The prisoners were dismissed, each with ten dollars in his pocket. An
agreement was formally drawn and signed in the
Escurial in which Philip gave Hawkins a pardon
for his misdemeanours in the West Indies, a patent
for a Spanish peerage, and a letter of credit for
40,000*l*. to put the privateers in a condition to do
service, and the money was actually paid by Philip's
London agent. Admitted as he now was to full
confidence, Fitzwilliam learnt all particulars of the
great plot. The story reads like a chapter from
Monte Cristo, and yet it is literally true.

It ends with a letter which I will read to you,
from Hawkins to Cecil :—

'My very good Lord,—It may please your
Honour to be advertised that Fitzwilliam is returned
from Spain, where his message was acceptably
received, both by the King himself, the Duke of
Feria, and others of the Privy Council. His
despatch and answer were with great expedition
and great countenance and favour of the King.
The Articles are sent to the Ambassador with
orders also for the money to be paid to me by him,
for the enterprise to proceed with all diligence.
The pretence is that my powers should join with
the Duke of Alva's powers, which he doth secretly
provide in Flanders, as well as with powers which
will come with the Duke of Medina Celi out of

Spain, and to invade this realm and set up the Queen of Scots. They have practised with us for the burning of Her Majesty's ships. Therefore there should be some good care had of them, but not as it may appear that anything is discovered. The King has sent a ruby of good price to the Queen of Scots, with letters also which in my judgment were good to be delivered. The letters be of no importance, but his message by word is to comfort her, and say that he hath now none other care but to place her in her own. It were good also that Fitzwilliam may have access to the Queen of Scots to render thanks for the delivery of the prisoners who are now at liberty. It will be a very good colour for your Lordship to confer with him more largely.

'I have sent your Lordship the copy of my pardon from the King of Spain, in the order and manner I have it, with my great titles and honours from the King, from which God deliver me. Their practices be very mischievous, and they be never idle; but God, I hope, will confound them and turn their devices on their own necks.

'Your Lordship's most faithfully to my power,
'JOHN HAWKINS.'

A few more words will conclude this curious episode. With the clue obtained by Fitzwilliam, and confessions twisted out of Story and other unwilling witnesses, the Ridolfi conspiracy was un-

ravelled before it broke into act. Norfolk lost his
head. The inferior miscreants were hanged. The
Queen of Scots had a narrow escape, and the Parliament accentuated the Protestant character of the
Church of England by embodying the Thirty-nine
Articles in a statute. Alva, who distrusted Ridolfi
from the first and disliked encouraging rebellion,
refused to interest himself further in Anglo-Catholic
plots. Elizabeth and Cecil could now breathe more
freely, and read Philip a lesson on the danger of
plotting against the lives of sovereigns.

So long as England and Spain were nominally
at peace, the presence of De la Mark and his
privateers in the Downs was at least indecent. A
committee of merchants at Bruges represented that
their losses by it amounted (as I said) to three
million ducats. Elizabeth, being now in comparative
safety, affected to listen to remonstrances, and orders
were sent down to De la Mark that he must prepare to leave. It is likely that both the Queen
and he understood each other, and that De la Mark
quite well knew where he was to go, and what he
was to do.

Alva now held every fortress in the Low
Countries, whether inland or on the coast. The
people were crushed. The duke's great statue
stood in the square at Antwerp as a symbol of the
annihilation of the ancient liberties of the Provinces. By sea alone the Prince of Orange still
continued the unequal struggle ; but if he was to

maintain himself as a sea power anywhere, he required a harbour of his own in his own country. Dover and the Thames had served for a time as a base of operations, but it could not last, and without a footing in Holland itself eventual success was impossible. All the Protestant world was interested in his fate, and De la Mark, with his miscellaneous gathering of Dutch, English, and Huguenot rovers, were ready for any desperate exploit.

The order was to leave Dover immediately, but it was not construed strictly. He lingered in the Downs for six weeks. At length, one morning at the end of March 1572, a Spanish convoy known to be richly loaded appeared in the Straits. De la Mark lifted anchor, darted out on it, seized two of the largest hulks, rifled them, flung their crews overboard, and chased the rest up Channel. A day or two after he suddenly showed himself off Brille, at the mouth of the Meuse. A boat was sent on shore with a note to the governor, demanding the instant surrender of the town to the admiral of the Prince of Orange. The inhabitants rose in enthusiasm ; the garrison was small, and the governor was obliged to comply. De la Mark took possession. A few priests and monks attempted resistance, but were put down without difficulty, and the leaders killed. The churches were cleared of their idols, and the mass replaced by the Calvinistic service. Cannon and stores, furnished from London, were landed, and Brille was made

impregnable before Alva had realised what had
happened to him. He is said to have torn his
beard for anger. Flushing followed suit. In a
week or two all the strongest places on the coast
had revolted, and the pirate fleet had laid the
foundation of the great Dutch Republic, which at
England's side was to strike out of Philip's hand
the sceptre of the seas, and to save the Protestant
religion.

We may think as we please of these Beggars of
the Ocean, these Norse corsairs come to life again
with the flavour of Genevan theology in them; but
for daring, for ingenuity, for obstinate determination
to be spiritually free or to die for it, the like of the
Protestant privateers of the sixteenth century has
been rarely met with in this world.

England rang with joy when the news came
that Brille was taken. Church bells pealed, and
bonfires blazed. Money poured across in streams.
Exiled families went back to their homes—which
were to be their homes once more—and the
Zealanders and Hollanders, entrenched among
their ditches, prepared for an amphibious conflict
with the greatest power then upon the earth.

LECTURE IV

DRAKE'S VOYAGE ROUND THE WORLD

I SUPPOSE some persons present have heard the
name of Lope de Vega, the Spanish poet of Philip
II.'s time. Very few of you probably know more of
him than his name, and yet he ought to have some
interest for us, as he was one of the many enthusiastic young Spaniards who sailed in the Great
Armada. He had been disappointed in some love
affair. He was an earnest Catholic. He wanted
distraction, and it is needless to say that he found
distraction enough in the English Channel to put
his love troubles out of his mind. His adventures
brought before him with some vividness the character of the nation with which his own country
was then in the death-grapple, especially the character of the great English seaman to whom the
Spaniards universally attributed their defeat. Lope
studied the exploits of Francis Drake from his first
appearance to his end, and he celebrated those
exploits, as England herself has never yet thought
it worth her while to do, by making him the hero of
an epic poem. There are heroes and heroes. Lope
de Vega's epic is called 'The Dragontea.' Drake

himself is the dragon, the ancient serpent of the Apo-
calypse. We English have been contented to allow
Drake a certain qualified praise. We admit that he
was a bold, dexterous sailor, that he did his country
good service at the Invasion. We allow that he
was a famous navigator, and sailed round the world,
which no one else had done before him. But—there
is always a but—of course he was a robber and a
corsair, and the only excuse for him is that he was
no worse than most of his contemporaries. To
Lope de Vega he was a great deal worse. He was
Satan himself, the incarnation of the Genius of
Evil, the arch-enemy of the Church of God.

It is worth while to look more particularly
at the figure of a man who appeared to the
Spaniards in such terrible proportions. I, for my
part, believe a time will come when we shall see
better than we see now what the Reformation was,
and what we owe to it, and these sea-captains of
Elizabeth will then form the subject of a great
English national epic as grand as the ' Odyssey.'

In my own poor way meanwhile I shall try in
these lectures to draw you a sketch of Drake and
his doings as they appear to myself. To-day I can
but give you a part of the rich and varied story,
but if all goes well I hope I may be able to continue
it at a future time.

I have not yet done with Sir John Hawkins.
We shall hear of him again. He became the
manager of Elizabeth's dockyards. He it was who

turned out the ships that fought Philip's fleet in
the Channel in such condition that not a hull
leaked, not a spar was sprung, not a rope parted at
an unseasonable moment, and this at a minimum
of cost. He served himself in the squadron which
he had equipped. He was one of the small group
of admirals who met that Sunday afternoon in the
cabin of the ark *Raleigh* and sent the fireships
down to stir Medina Sidonia out of his anchorage
at Calais. He was a child of the sea, and at sea
he died, sinking at last into his mother's arms.
But of this hereafter. I must speak now of his
still more illustrious kinsman, Francis Drake.

I told you the other day generally who Drake
was and where he came from ; how he went to sea
as a boy, found favour with his master, became
early an owner of his own ship, sticking steadily
to trade. You hear nothing of him in connection
with the Channel pirates. It was not till he was
five-and-twenty that he was tempted by Hawkins
into the negro-catching business, and of this one
experiment was enough. He never tried it again.

The portraits of him vary very much, as indeed
it is natural that they should, for most of those
which pass for Drake were not meant for Drake at
all. It is the fashion in this country, and a very
bad fashion, when we find a remarkable portrait
with no name authoritatively attached to it, to
christen it at random after some eminent man, and
there it remains to perplex or mislead.

G

The best likeness of Drake that I know is an
engraving in Sir William Stirling-Maxwell's collection of sixteenth-century notabilities, representing
him, as a scroll says at the foot of the plate, at the
age of forty-three. The face is round, the forehead
broad and full, with the short brown hair curling
crisply on either side. The eyebrows are highly
arched, the eyes firm, clear, and open. I cannot
undertake for the colour, but I should judge they
would be dark grey, like an eagle's. The nose is
short and thick, the mouth and chin hid by a heavy
moustache on the upper lip, and a close-clipped
beard well spread over chin and cheek. The
expression is good-humoured, but absolutely in-
flexible, not a weak line to be seen. He was of
middle height, powerfully built, perhaps too powerfully for grace, unless the quilted doublet in which
the artist has dressed him exaggerates his breadth.

I have seen another portrait of him, with pretensions to authenticity, in which he appears with
a slighter figure, eyes dark, full, thoughtful, and
stern, a sailor's cord about his neck with a whistle
attached to it, and a ring into which a thumb is
carelessly thrust, the weight of the arms resting on
it, as if in a characteristic attitude. Evidently
this is a carefully drawn likeness of some remarkable seaman of the time. I should like to believe
it to be Drake, but I can feel no certainty about it.

We left him returned home in the *Judith* from
San Juan de Ulloa, a ruined man. He had never

injured the Spaniards. He had gone out with his
cousin merely to trade, and he had met with a
hearty reception from the settlers wherever he had
been. A Spanish admiral had treacherously set
upon him and his kinsman, destroyed half their
vessels, and robbed them of all that they had.
They had left a hundred of their comrades behind
them, for whose fate they might fear the worst.
Drake thenceforth considered Spanish property as
fair game till he had made up his own losses. He
waited quietly for four years till he had re-established himself, and then prepared to try fortune
again in a more daring form.

The ill-luck at San Juan de Ulloa had risen
from loose tongues. There had been too much talk
about it. Too many parties had been concerned.
The Spanish Government had notice and were
prepared. Drake determined to act for himself,
have no partners, and keep his own secret. He
found friends to trust him with money without
asking for explanations. The Plymouth sailors
were eager to take their chance with him. His
force was absurdly small: a sloop or brigantine
of a hundred tons, which he called the *Dragon*
(perhaps, like Lope de Vega, playing on his own
name), and two small pinnaces. With these he
left Plymouth in the fall of the summer of 1572.
He had ascertained that Philip's gold and silver
from the Peruvian mines was landed at Panama,
carried across the isthmus on mules' backs on the

line of M. de Lesseps' canal, and re-shipped at
Nombre de Dios, at the mouth of the Chagre River.

He told no one where he was going. He was
no more communicative than necessary after his
return, and the results, rather than the particulars,
of his adventure are all that can be certainly known.
Discretion told him to keep his counsel, and he
kept it.

The Drake family published an account of this
voyage in the middle of the next century, but
obviously mythical, in parts demonstrably false, and
nowhere to be depended on. It can be made out,
however, that he did go to Nombre de Dios, that
he found his way into the town, and saw stores of
bullion there which he would have liked to carry
off but could not. A romantic story of a fight in
the town I disbelieve, first because his numbers
were so small that to try force would have been
absurd, and next because if there had been really
anything like a battle an alarm would have been
raised in the neighbourhood, and it is evident that
no alarm was given. In the woods were parties of
runaway slaves, who were called Cimarons. It
was to these that Drake addressed himself, and
they volunteered to guide him where he could surprise the treasure convoy on the way from Panama.
His movements were silent and rapid. One interesting incident is mentioned which is authentic.
The Cimarons took him through the forest to the
watershed from which the streams flow to both

oceans. Nothing could be seen through the jungle of undergrowth; but Drake climbed a tall tree, saw from the top of it the Pacific glittering below him, and made a vow that one day he would himself sail a ship in those waters.

For the present he had immediate work on hand. His guides kept their word. They led him to the track from Panama, and he had not long to wait before the tinkling was heard of the mule bells as they were coming up the pass. There was no suspicion of danger, not the faintest. The mule train had but its ordinary guard, who fled at the first surprise. The immense booty fell all into Drake's hands—gold, jewels, silver bars—and got with much ease, as Prince Hal said at Gadshill. The silver they buried, as too heavy for transport. The gold, pearls, rubies, emeralds, and diamonds they carried down straight to their ship. The voyage home went prosperously. The spoils were shared among the adventurers, and they had no reason to complain. They were wise enough to hold their tongues, and Drake was in a condition to look about him and prepare for bigger enterprises.

Rumours got abroad, spite of reticence. Imagination was high in flight just then; rash amateurs thought they could make their fortunes in the same way, and tried it, to their sorrow. A sort of inflation can be traced in English sailors' minds as their work expanded. Even Hawkins—the clear,

practical Hawkins—was infected. This was not
in Drake's line. He kept to prose and fact. He
studied the globe. He examined all the charts that
he could get. He became known to the Privy
Council and the Queen, and prepared for an enterprise which would make his name and frighten
Philip in earnest.

The ships which the Spaniards used on the
Pacific were usually built on the spot. But Magellan was known to have gone by the Horn, and
where a Portuguese could go an Englishman could
go. Drake proposed to try. There was a party in
Elizabeth's Council against these adventures, and in
favour of peace with Spain; but Elizabeth herself
was always for enterprises of pith and moment. She
was willing to help, and others of her Council were
willing too, provided their names were not to
appear. The responsibility was to be Drake's own.
Again the vessels in which he was preparing to
tempt fortune seem preposterously small. The
Pelican, or *Golden Hinde*, which belonged to Drake
himself, was called but 120 tons, at best no larger
than a modern racing yawl, though perhaps no
racing yawl ever left White's yard better found
for the work which she had to do. The next, the
Elizabeth, of London, was said to be eighty tons;
a small pinnace of twelve tons, in which we should
hardly risk a summer cruise round the Land's End,
with two sloops or frigates of fifty and thirty tons,
made the rest. The *Elizabeth* was commanded

by Captain Winter, a Queen's officer, and perhaps a son of the old admiral.

We may credit Drake with knowing what he was about. He and his comrades were carrying their lives in their hands. If they were taken they would be inevitably hanged. Their safety depended on speed of sailing, and specially on the power of working fast to windward, which the heavy square-rigged ships could not do. The crews all told were 160 men and boys. Drake had his brother John with him. Among his officers were the chaplain, Mr. Fletcher, another minister of some kind who spoke Spanish, and in one of the sloops a mysterious Mr. Doughty. Who Mr. Doughty was, and why he was sent out, is uncertain. When an expedition of consequence was on hand, the Spanish party in the Cabinet usually attached to it some second in command whose business was to defeat the object. When Drake went to Cadiz in after years to singe King Philip's beard, he had a colleague sent with him whom he had to lock into his cabin before he could get to his work. So far as I can make out, Mr. Doughty had a similar commission. On this occasion secrecy was impossible. It was generally known that Drake was going to the Pacific through Magellan Straits, to act afterwards on his own judgment. The Spanish ambassador, now Don Bernardino de Mendoza, in informing Philip of what was intended, advised him to send out orders for the instant sinking of every English ship, and the execution of every English sailor, that appeared on either side the isthmus in West Indian waters. The orders were despatched, but so impossible it seemed that an English pirate could reach the Pacific, that the attention was confined to the Caribbean Sea, and not a hint of alarm was sent across to the other side.

On November 15, 1577, the *Pelican* and her consort sailed out of Plymouth Sound. The elements frowned on their start. On the second day they were caught in a winter gale. The *Pelican* sprung her mainmast, and they put back to refit and repair. But Drake defied auguries. Before the middle of December all was again in order. The weather mended, and with a fair wind and smooth water they made a fast run across the Bay of Biscay and down the coast to the Cape de Verde Islands. There taking up the north-east trades, they struck across the Atlantic, crossed the line, and made the South American continent in latitude 33° South. They passed the mouth of the Plate River, finding to their astonishment fresh water at the ship's side in fifty-four fathoms. All seemed so far going well, when one morning Mr. Doughty's sloop was missing, and he along with her. Drake, it seemed, had already reason to distrust Doughty, and guessed the direction in which he had gone. The *Marigold* was sent in pursuit, and he was overtaken and brought back. To prevent a repetition of such a performance, Drake took the sloop's

stores out of her, burnt her, distributed the crew
through the other vessels, and took Mr. Doughty
under his own charge. On June 20 they reached
Port St. Julian, on the coast of Patagonia.
They had been long on the way, and the southern
winter had come round, and they had to delay
further to make more particular inquiry into
Doughty's desertion. An ominous and strange
spectacle met their eyes as they entered the harbour. In that utterly desolate spot a skeleton was
hanging on a gallows, the bones picked clean by
the vultures. It was one of Magellan's crew who
had been executed there for mutiny fifty years
before. The same fate was to befall the unhappy
Englishman who had been guilty of the same fault.
Without the strictest discipline it was impossible
for the enterprise to succeed, and Doughty had been
guilty of worse than disobedience. We are told
briefly that his conduct was found tending to con-
tention, and threatening the success of the voyage.
Part he was said to have confessed; part was
proved against him—one knows not what. A court
was formed out of the crew. He was tried, as near
as circumstances allowed, according to English
usage. He was found guilty, and was sentenced
to die. He made no complaint, or none of which
a record is preserved. He asked for the Sacrament,
which was of course allowed, and Drake himself
communicated with him. They then kissed each
other, and the unlucky wretch took leave of his

comrades, laid his head on the block, and so ended. His offence can be only guessed; but the suspicious curiosity about his fate which was shown afterwards by Mendoza makes it likely that he was in Spanish pay. The ambassador cross-questioned Captain Winter very particularly about him, and we learn one remarkable fact from Mendoza's letters not mentioned by any English writer, that Drake was himself the executioner, choosing to bear the entire responsibility.

'This done,' writes an eyewitness, 'the general made divers speeches to the whole company, persuading us to unity, obedience, and regard of our voyage, and for the better confirmation thereof willed every man the Sunday following to prepare himself to receive the Communion as Christian brothers and friends ought to do, which was done in very reverent sort; and so with good contentment every man went about his business.'

You must take this last incident into your conception of Drake's character, think of it how you please.

It was now midwinter, the stormiest season of the year, and they remained for six weeks in Port St. Julian. They burnt the twelve-ton pinnace, as too small for the work they had now before them, and there remained only the *Pelican*, the *Elizabeth*, and the *Marigold*. In cold wild weather they weighed at last, and on August 20 made the opening of Magellan's Straits. The passage is seventy miles long, tortuous and dangerous. They had no charts. The ships' boats led, taking soundings as they advanced. Icy mountains overhung them on either side ; heavy snow fell below. They brought up occasionally at an island to rest the men, and let them kill a few seals and penguins to give them fresh food. Everything they saw was new, wild, and wonderful.

Having to feel their way, they were three weeks in getting through. They had counted on reaching the Pacific that the worst of their work was over, and that they could run north at once into warmer and calmer latitudes. The peaceful ocean, when they entered it, proved the stormiest they had ever sailed on. A fierce westerly gale drove them 600 miles to the south-east outside the Horn. It had been supposed, hitherto, that Tierra del Fuego was solid land to the South Pole, and that the Straits were the only communication between the Atlantic and the Pacific. They now learnt the true shape and character of the Western Continent. In the latitude of Cape Horn a westerly gale blows for ever round the globe ; the waves the highest anywhere known. The *Marigold* went down in the tremendous encounter. Captain Winter, in the *Elizabeth*, made his way back into Magellan's Straits. There he lay for three weeks, lighting fires nightly to show Drake where he was, but no Drake appeared. They had agreed, if separated, to meet on the coast in the latitude of

Valparaiso; but Winter was chicken-hearted, or else traitorous like Doughty, and sore, we are told, 'against the mariners' will,' when the three weeks were out, he sailed away for England, where he reported that all the ships were lost but the *Pelican*, and that the *Pelican* was probably lost too.

Drake had believed better of Winter, and had not expected to be so deserted. He had himself taken refuge among the islands which form the Cape, waiting for the spring and milder weather. He used the time in making surveys, and observing the habits of the native Patagonians, whom he found a tough race, going naked amidst ice and snow. The days lengthened, and the sea smoothed at last. He then sailed for Valparaiso, hoping to meet Winter there, as he had arranged. At Valparaiso there was no Winter, but there was in the port instead a great galleon just come in from Peru. The galleon's crew took him for a Spaniard, hoisted their colours, and beat their drums. The *Pelican* shot alongside. The English sailors in high spirits leapt on board. A Plymouth lad who could speak Spanish knocked down the first man he met with an 'Abajo, perro!' 'Down, you dog, down!' No life was taken; Drake never hurt man if he could help it. The crew crossed themselves, jumped overboard, and swam ashore. The prize was examined. Four hundred pounds' weight of gold was found in her, besides other plunder.

The galleon being disposed of, Drake and his

men pulled ashore to look at the town. The people had all fled. In the church they found a chalice, two cruets, and an altar-cloth, which were made over to the chaplain to improve his Communion furniture. A few pipes of wine and a Greek pilot who knew the way to Lima completed the booty.

' Shocking piracy,' you will perhaps say. But what Drake was doing would have been all right and good service had war been declared, and the essence of things does not alter with the form. In essence there *was* war, deadly war, between Philip and Elizabeth. Even later, when the Armada sailed, there had been no formal declaration. The reality is the important part of the matter. It was but stroke for stroke, and the English arm proved the stronger.

Still hoping to find Winter in advance of him, Drake went on next to Tarapaca, where silver from the Andes mines was shipped for Panama. At Tarapaca there was the same unconsciousness of danger. The silver bars lay piled on the quay, the muleteers who had brought them were sleeping peacefully in the sunshine at their side. The muleteers were left to their slumbers. The bars were lifted into the English boats. A train of mules or llamas came in at the moment with a second load as rich as the first. This, too, went into the *Pelican's* hold. The bullion taken at Tarapaca was worth near half a million ducats.

Still there were no news of Winter. Drake

began to realise that he was now entirely alone, and had only himself and his own crew to depend on. There was nothing to do but to go through with it, danger adding to the interest. Arica was the next point visited. Half a hundred blocks of silver were picked up at Arica. After Arica came Lima, the chief depôt of all, where the grandest haul was looked for. At Lima, alas! they were just too late. Twelve great hulks lay anchored there. The sails were unbent, the men were ashore. They contained nothing but some chests of reals and a few bales of silk and linen. But a thirteenth, called by the gods *Our Lady of the Conception*, called by men *Cacafuego*, a name incapable of translation, had sailed a few days before for the isthmus, with the whole produce of the Lima mines for the season. Her ballast was silver, her cargo gold and emeralds and rubies.

Drake deliberately cut the cables of the ships in the roads, that they might drive ashore and be unable to follow him. The *Pelican* spread her wings, every feather of them, and sped away in pursuit. He would know the *Cacafuego*, so he learnt at Lima, by the peculiar cut of her sails. The first man who caught sight of her was promised a gold chain for his reward. A sail was seen on the second day. It was not the chase, but it was worth stopping for. Eighty pounds' weight of gold was found, and a great gold crucifix, set with emeralds said to be as large as pigeon's eggs.

They took the kernel. They left the shell. Still
on and on. We learn from the Spanish accounts
that the Viceroy of Lima, as soon as he recovered
from his astonishment, despatched ships in pursuit.
They came up with the last plundered vessel, heard
terrible tales of the rovers' strength, and went back
for a larger force. The *Pelican* meanwhile went
along upon her course for 800 miles. At length,
when in the latitude of Quito and close under the
shore, the *Cacafuego's* peculiar sails were sighted,
and the gold chain was claimed. There she was,
freighted with the fruit of Aladdin's garden, going
lazily along a few miles ahead. Care was needed
in approaching her. If she guessed the *Pelican's*
character, she would run in upon the land and they
would lose her. It was afternoon. The sun was
still above the horizon, and Drake meant to wait
till night, when the breeze would be off the shore,
as in the tropics it always is.

The *Pelican* sailed two feet to the *Cacafuego's*
one. Drake filled his empty wine-skins with water
and trailed them astern to stop his way. The
chase supposed that she was followed by some
heavy-loaded trader, and, wishing for company on
a lonely voyage, she slackened sail and waited for
him to come up. At length the sun went down
into the ocean, the rosy light faded from off the
snows of the Andes; and when both ships had become
invisible from the shore, the skins were hauled in,
the night wind rose, and the water began to ripple

under the *Pelican's* bows. The *Cacafuego* was
swiftly overtaken, and when within a cable's length
a voice hailed her to put her head into the wind.
The Spanish commander, not understanding so
strange an order, held on his course. A broadside
brought down his mainyard, and a flight of arrows
rattled on his deck. He was himself wounded.
In a few minutes he was a prisoner, and *Our Lady
of the Conception* and her precious freight were in
the corsair's power. The wreck was cut away;
the ship was cleared; a prize crew was put on
board. Both vessels turned their heads to the sea.
At daybreak no land was to be seen, and the examination of the prize began. The full value was
never acknowledged. The invoice, if there was
one, was destroyed. The accurate figures were
known only to Drake and Queen Elizabeth. A
published schedule acknowledged to twenty tons of
silver bullion, thirteen chests of silver coins, and a
hundredweight of gold, but there were gold nuggets
besides in indefinite quantity, and 'a great store'
of pearls, emeralds, and diamonds. The Spanish
Government proved a loss of a million and a half
of ducats, excluding what belonged to private
persons. The total capture was immeasurably
greater.

Drake, we are told, was greatly satisfied. He
thought it prudent to stay in the neighbourhood no
longer than necessary. He went north with all
sail set, taking his prize along with him. The

master, San Juan de Anton, was removed on board
the *Pelican* to have his wound attended to. He
remained as Drake's guest for a week, and sent in
a report of what he observed to the Spanish Government. One at least of Drake's party spoke excellent Spanish. This person took San Juan over the
ship. She showed signs, San Juan said, of rough
service, but was still in fine condition, with ample
arms, spare rope, mattocks, carpenters' tools of all
descriptions. There were eighty-five men on board
all told, fifty of them men-of-war, the rest young
fellows, ship-boys and the like. Drake himself was
treated with great reverence; a sentinel stood
always at his cabin door. He dined alone with
music.

No mystery was made of the *Pelican's* exploits.
The chaplain showed San Juan the crucifix set
with emeralds, and asked him if he could seriously
believe that to be God. San Juan asked Drake
how he meant to go home. Drake showed him a
globe with three courses traced on it. There was
the way that he had come, there was the way by
China and the Cape of Good Hope, and there was
a third way which he did not explain. San Juan
asked if Spain and England were at war. Drake
said he had a commission from the Queen. His
captures were for her, not for himself. He added
afterwards that the Viceroy of Mexico had robbed
him and his kinsman, and he was making good his
losses.

Then, touching the point of the sore, he said,
' I know the Viceroy will send for thee to inform
himself of my proceedings. Tell him he shall
do well to put no more Englishmen to death,
and to spare those he has in his hands, for if he
do execute them I will hang 2,000 Spaniards and
send him their heads.'

After a week's detention San Juan and his men
were restored to the empty *Cacafuego*, and allowed
to go. On their way back they fell in with the two
cruisers sent in pursuit from Lima, reinforced by a
third from Panama. They were now fully armed;
they went in chase, and according to their own
account came up with the *Pelican*. But, like
Lope de Vega, they seemed to have been terrified
at Drake as a sort of devil. They confessed that
they dared not attack him, and again went back
for more assistance. The Viceroy abused them as
cowards, arrested the officers, despatched others
again with peremptory orders to seize Drake, even
if he was the devil, but by that time their ques
tionable visitor had flown. They found nothing,
perhaps to their relief.

A despatch went instantly across the Atlantic to
Philip. One squadron was sent off from Cadiz to
watch the Straits of Magellan, and another to patrol
the Caribbean Sea. It was thought that Drake's
third way was no seaway at all, that he meant to
leave the *Pelican* at Darien, carry his plunder
over the mountains, and build a ship at Honduras

to take him home. His real idea was that he might
hit off the passage to the north of which Frobisher
and Davis thought they had found the eastern
entrance. He stood on towards California, picking
up an occasional straggler in the China trade, with
silk, porcelain, gold, and emeralds. Fresh water
was a necessity. He put in at Guatulco for it, and
his proceedings were humorously prompt. The
alcaldes at Guatulco were in session trying a batch
of negroes. An English boat's crew appeared in
court, tied the alcaldes hand and foot, and carried
them off to the *Pelican*, there to remain as hostages till the water-casks were filled.

North again he fell in with a galleon carrying
out a new Governor to the Philippines. The
Governor was relieved of his boxes and his jewels,
and then, says one of the party, 'Our General,
thinking himself in respect of his private injuries
received from the Spaniards, as also their contempt
and indignities offered to our country and Prince,
sufficiently satisfied and revenged, and supposing
her Majesty would rest contented with this service,
began to consider the best way home.' The first
necessity was a complete overhaul of the ship.
Before the days of copper sheathing weeds grew
thick under water. Barnacles formed in clusters,
stopping the speed, and sea-worms bored through
the planking. Twenty thousand miles lay between
the *Pelican* and Plymouth Sound, and Drake was
not a man to run idle chances. Still holding his

north course till he had left the furthest Spanish settlement far to the south, he put into Canoas Bay in California, laid the *Pelican* ashore, set up forge and workshop, and repaired and re-rigged her with a month's labour from stem to stern. With every rope new set up and new canvas on every yard, he started again on April 16, 1579, and continued up the coast to Oregon. The air grew cold though it was summer. The men felt it from having been so long in the tropics, and dropped out of health. There was still no sign of a passage. If passage there was, Drake perceived that it must be of enormous length. Magellan's Straits, he guessed, would be watched for him, so he decided on the route by the Cape of Good Hope. In the Philippine ship he had found a chart of the Indian Archipelago. With the help of this and his own skill he hoped to find his way. He went down again to San Francisco, landed there, found the soil teeming with gold, made acquaintance with an Indian king who hated the Spaniards and wished to become an English subject. But Drake had no leisure to annex new territories. Avoiding the course from Mexico to the Philippines, he made a direct course to the Moluccas, and brought up again at the Island of Celebes. Here the *Pelican* was a second time docked and scraped. The crew had a month's rest among the fireflies and vampires of the tropical forest. Leaving Celebes, they entered on the most perilous part of the whole voyage. They wound

their way among coral reefs and low islands
scarcely visible above the water-line. In their
chart the only outlet marked into the Indian Ocean
was by the Straits of Malacca. But Drake guessed
rightly that there must be some nearer opening,
and felt his way looking for it along the coast of
Java. Spite of all his care, he was once on the
edge of destruction. One evening as night was
closing in a grating sound was heard under the
Pelican's keel. In another moment she was hard
and fast on a reef. The breeze was light and the
water smooth, or the world would have heard no
more of Francis Drake. She lay immovable till
daybreak. At dawn the position was seen not to be
entirely desperate. Drake himself showed all the
qualities of a great commander. Cannon were
thrown over and cargo that was not needed. In
the afternoon, the wind changing, the lightened
vessel lifted off the rocks and was saved. The hull
was uninjured, thanks to the Californian repairs.
All on board had behaved well with the one
exception of Mr. Fletcher, the chaplain. Mr.
Fletcher, instead of working like a man, had whined
about Divine retribution for the execution of
Doughty.

For the moment Drake passed it over. A few
days after, they passed out through the Straits of
Sunda, where they met the great ocean swell,
Homer's μέγα κῦμα θαλάσσης, and they knew then
that all was well.

There was now time to call Mr. Fletcher to account. It was no business of the chaplain to discourage and dispirit men in a moment of danger, and a court was formed to sit upon him. An English captain on his own deck represents the sovereign, and is head of Church as well as State. Mr. Fletcher was brought to the forecastle, where Drake, sitting on a sea-chest with a pair of *pantoufles* in his hand, excommunicated him, pronounced him cut off from the Church of God, given over to the devil for the chastising of his flesh, and left him chained by the leg to a ring-bolt to repent of his cowardice.

In the general good-humour punishment could not be of long duration. The next day the poor chaplain had his absolution and returned to his berth and his duty. The *Pelican* met with no more adventures. Sweeping in fine clear weather round the Cape of Good Hope, she touched once for water at Sierra Leone, and finally sailed in triumph into Plymouth Harbour, where she had been long given up for lost, having traced the first furrow round the globe. Winter had come home eighteen months before, but could report nothing. The news of the doings on the American coast had reached England through Madrid. The Spanish ambassador had been furious. It was known that Spanish squadrons had been sent in search. Complications would arise if Drake brought his plunder home, and timid politicians hoped that he was at the bottom of the sea. But here he was, actually arrived with a monarch's ransom in his hold.

English sympathy with an extraordinary exploit is always irresistible. Shouts of applause rang through the country, and Elizabeth, every bit of her an Englishwoman, felt with her subjects. She sent for Drake to London, made him tell his story over and over again, and was never weary of listening to him. As to injury to Spain, Philip had lighted a fresh insurrection in Ireland, which had cost her dearly in lives and money. For Philip to demand compensation of England on the score of justice was a thing to make the gods laugh.

So thought the Queen. So unfortunately did not think some members of her Council, Lord Burghley among them. Mendoza was determined that Drake should be punished and the spoils disgorged, or else that he would force Elizabeth upon the world as the confessed protectress of piracy Burghley thought that, as things stood, some satisfaction (or the form of it) would have to be made.

Elizabeth hated paying back as heartily as Falstaff, nor had she the least intention of throwing to the wolves a gallant Englishman, with whose achievements the world was ringing. She was obliged to allow the treasure to be registered by a responsible official, and an account rendered to Mendoza; but for all that she meant to keep her own share of the spoils. She meant, too, that Drake and his brave crew should not go unrewarded. Drake himself should have ten thousand pounds at least.

Her action was eminently characteristic of her. On the score of real justice there was no doubt at all how matters stood between herself and Philip, who had tried to dethrone and kill her.

The *Pelican* lay still at Plymouth with the bullion and jewels untouched. She directed that it should be landed and scheduled. She trusted the business to Edmund Tremayne, of Sydenham, a neighbouring magistrate, on whom she could depend. She told him not to be too inquisitive, and she allowed Drake to go back and arrange the cargo before the examination was made. Let me now read you a letter from Tremayne himself to Sir Francis Walsingham :—

' To give you some understanding how I have proceeded with Mr. Drake : I have at no time entered into the account to know more of the value of the treasure than he made me acquainted with ; and to say truth I persuaded him to impart to me no more than need, for so I saw him commanded in her Majesty's behalf that he should reveal the certainty to no man living. I have only taken notice of so much as he *has* revealed, and the same I have seen to be weighed, registered, and packed. And to observe her Majesty's commands for the ten thousand pounds, we agreed he should take it

out of the portion that was landed secretly, and to
remove the same out of the place before my son
Henry and I should come to the weighing and
registering of what was left; and so it was done,
and no creature living by me made privy to it but
himself; and myself no privier to it than as you
may perceive by this.

'I see nothing to charge Mr. Drake further than
he is inclined to charge himself, and withal I must
say he is inclined to advance the value to be
delivered to her Majesty, and seeking in general
to recompense all men that have been in the case
dealers with him. As I dare take an oath, he will
rather diminish his own portion than leave any
of them unsatisfied. And for his mariners and
followers I have seen here as eye-witness, and have
heard with my ears, such certain signs of goodwill
as I cannot yet see that any of them will leave his
company. The whole course of his voyage hath
showed him to be of great valour; but my hap
has been to see some particulars, and namely in
this discharge of his company, as doth assure me
that he is a man of great government, and that
by the rules of God and his book, so as proceed-
ing on such foundation his doings cannot but
prosper.'

The result of it all was that deductions were
made from the capture equivalent to the property
which Drake and Hawkins held themselves to have
been treacherously plundered of at San Juan de

Ulloa, with perhaps other liberal allowances for the cost of recovery. An account on part of what remained was then given to Mendoza. It was not returned to him or to Philip, but was laid up in the Tower till the final settlement of Philip's and the Queen's claims on each other—the cost, for one thing, of the rebellion in Ireland. Commissioners met and argued and sat on ineffectually till the Armada came and the discussion ended, and the talk of restitution was over. Meanwhile, opinion varied about Drake's own doings as it has varied since. Elizabeth listened spellbound to his adventures, sent for him to London again, and walked with him publicly about the parks and gardens. She gave him a second ten thousand pounds. The *Pelican* was sent round to Deptford; a royal banquet was held on board, Elizabeth attended and Drake was knighted. Mendoza clamoured for the treasure in the Tower to be given up to him; Walsingham wished to give it to the Prince of Orange; Leicester and his party in the Council, who had helped to fit Drake out, thought it ought to be divided among themselves, and unless Mendoza lies they offered to share it with him if he would agree to a private arrangement. Mendoza says he answered that he would give twice as much to chastise such a bandit as Drake. Elizabeth thought it should be kept as a captured pawn in the game, and so in fact it remained after the deductions which we have seen had been made.

Drake was lavish of his presents. He presented the Queen with a diamond cross and a coronet set with splendid emeralds. He gave Bromley, the Lord Chancellor, 800 dollars' worth of silver plate, and as much more to other members of the Council. The Queen wore her coronet on New Year's Day; the Chancellor was content to decorate his sideboard at the cost of the Catholic King. Burghley and Sussex declined the splendid temptation; they said they could accept no such precious gifts from a man whose fortune had been made by plunder.

Burghley lived to see better into Drake's value. Meanwhile, what now are we, looking back over our history, to say of these things—the Channel privateering; the seizure of Alva's army money; the sharp practice of Hawkins with the Queen of Scots and King Philip; or this amazing performance of Sir Francis Drake in a vessel no larger than a second-rate yacht of a modern noble lord?

Resolution, daring, professional skill, all historians allow to these men; but, like Burghley, they regard what they did as piracy, not much better, if at all better, than the later exploits of Morgan and Kidd. So cried the Catholics who wished Elizabeth's ruin; so cried Lope de Vega and King Philip. In milder language the modern philosopher repeats the unfavourable verdict, rejoices that he lives in an age when such doings are impossible, and apologises faintly for the excesses of an imperfect age. May I remind the philosopher that we live in an age when other things have also happily become impossible, and that if he and his friends were liable when they went abroad for their summer tours to be snapped by the familiars of the Inquisition, whipped, burnt alive, or sent to the galleys, he would perhaps think more leniently of any measures by which that respectable institution and its masters might be induced to treat philosophers with greater consideration?

Again, remember Dr. Johnson's warning, Beware of cant. In that intensely serious century men were more occupied with the realities than the forms of things. By encouraging rebellion in England and Ireland, by burning so many scores of poor English seamen and merchants in fools' coats at Seville, the King of Spain had given Elizabeth a hundred occasions for declaring war against him. Situated as she was, with so many disaffected Catholic subjects, she could not *begin* a war on such a quarrel. She had to use such resources as she had, and of these resources the best was a splendid race of men who were not afraid to do for her at their own risk what commissioned officers would and might have justly done had formal war been declared, men who defeated the national enemy with materials conquered from himself, who were devoted enough to dispense with the personal security which the sovereign's commission would have extended to prisoners of war, and face the certainty of being hanged if they were taken.

Yes; no doubt by the letter of the law of nations Drake and Hawkins were corsairs of the same stuff as Ulysses, as the rovers of Norway.   But the common-sense of Europe saw through the form to the substance which lay below it, and the instinct of their countrymen gave them a place among the fighting heroes of England, from which I do not think they will be deposed by the eventual verdict of history.

LECTURE V

PARTIES IN THE STATE

On December 21, 1585, a remarkable scene took place in the English House of Commons. The Prince of Orange, after many attempts had failed, had been successfully disposed of in the Low Countries. A fresh conspiracy had just been discovered for a Catholic insurrection in England, supported by a foreign invasion; the object of which was to dethrone Elizabeth and to give her crown to Mary Stuart. The Duke of Alva, at the time of the Ridolfi plot, had pointed out as a desirable preliminary, if the invasion was to succeed, the assassination of the Queen of England. The succession being undecided, he had calculated that the confusion would paralyse resistance, and the notorious favour with which Mary Stuart's pretensions were regarded by a powerful English party would ensure her an easy victory were Elizabeth once removed. But this was an indispensable condition. It had become clear at last that so long as Elizabeth was alive Philip would not willingly sanction the landing of a Spanish army on English shores. Thus, among the more ardent Catholics, especially the refugees at the Seminary at Rheims, a crown in heaven was held out to any spiritual knight-errant who would remove the obstacle. The enterprise itself was not a difficult one. Elizabeth was aware of her danger, but she was personally fearless. She refused to distrust the Catholics. Her household was full of them. She admitted anyone to her presence who desired a private interview. Dr. Parry, a member of Parliament, primed by encouragements from the Cardinal of Como and the Vatican, had undertaken to risk his life to win the glorious prize. He introduced himself into the palace, properly provided with arms. He professed to have information of importance to give. The Queen received him repeatedly. Once he was alone with her in the palace garden, and was on the point of killing her, when he was awed, as he said, by the likeness to her father. Parry was discovered and hanged, but Elizabeth refused to take warning. When there were so many aspirants for the honour of removing Jezebel, and Jezebel was so easy of approach, it was felt that one would at last succeed; and the loyal part of the nation, led by Lord Burghley, formed themselves into an association to protect a life so vital to them and apparently so indifferent to herself.

The subscribers bound themselves to pursue to the death all manner of persons who should attempt or consent to anything to the harm of her Majesty's person; never to allow or submit to any pretended

successor by whom or for whom such detestable
act should be attempted or committed; but to
pursue such persons to death and act the utmost
revenge upon them.

The bond in its first form was a visible creation
of despair. It implied a condition of things in
which order would have ceased to exist. The
lawyers, who, it is curious to observe, were
generally in Mary Stuart's interest, vehemently
objected; yet so passionate was public feeling
that it was signed throughout the kingdom, and
Parliament was called to pass an Act which would
secure the same object. Mary Stuart, at any rate,
was not to benefit by the crimes either of herself or
her admirers. It was provided that if the realm
was invaded, or a rebellion instigated by or for any
one pretending a title to the crown after the Queen's
death, such pretender should be disqualified for
ever. In the event of the Queen's assassination the
government was to devolve on a Committee of
Peers and Privy Councillors, who were to examine
the particulars of the murder and execute the
perpetrators and their accomplices; while, with a
significant allusion, all Jesuits and seminary priests
were required to leave the country instantly, under
pain of death.

The House of Commons was heaving with
emotion when the Act was sent up to the Peers.
To give expression to their burning feelings Sir
Christopher Hatton proposed that before they

separated they should join him in a prayer for
the Queen's preservation. The 400 members
all rose, and knelt on the floor of the House, re-
peating Hatton's words after him, sentence by
sentence.

Jesuits and seminary priests! Attempts have
been made to justify the conspiracies against
Elizabeth from what is called the persecution of
the innocent enthusiasts who came from Rheims
to preach the Catholic faith to the English people.
Popular writers and speakers dwell on the executions of Campian and his friends as worse than the
Smithfield burnings, and amidst general admira-
tion and approval these martyred saints have been
lately canonised. Their mission, it is said, was
purely religious. Was it so ? The chief article in
the religion which they came to teach was the duty
of obedience to the Pope, who had excommunicated
the Queen, had absolved her subjects from their
allegiance, and, by a relaxation of the Bull, had
permitted them to pretend to loyalty *ad illud
tempus*, till a Catholic army of deliverance should
arrive. A Pope had sent a legate to Ireland, and
was at that moment stirring up a bloody insurrection there.

But what these seminary priests were, and what
their object was, will best appear from an account
of the condition of England, drawn up for the use
of the Pope and Philip, by Father Parsons, who was
himself at the head of the mission. The date of it

I

is 1585, almost simultaneous with the scene in Parliament which I have just been describing. The English refugees, from Cardinal Pole downwards, were the most active and passionate preachers of a Catholic crusade against England. They failed, but they have revenged themselves in history. Pole, Sanders, Allen, and Parsons have coloured all that we suppose ourselves to know of Henry VIII. and Elizabeth. What I am about to read to you does not differ essentially from what we have already heard from these persons ; but it is new, and, being intended for practical guidance, is complete in its way. It comes from the Spanish archives, and is not therefore open to suspicion. Parsons, as you know, was a Fellow of Balliol before his conversion ; Allen was a Fellow of Oriel, and Sanders of New College. An Oxford Church of England education is an excellent thing, and beautiful characters have been formed in the Catholic universities abroad ; but as the elements of dynamite are innocent in themselves, yet when fused together produce effects no one would have dreamt of, so Oxford and Rome, when they have run together, have always generated a somewhat furious compound.

Parsons describes his statement as a ' brief note on the present condition of England,' from which may be inferred the ease and opportuneness of the holy enterprise. ' England,' he says, ' contains fifty-two counties, of which forty are well inclined to the Catholic faith. Heretics in these are few, and are hated by all ranks. The remaining twelve are infected more or less, but even in these the Catholics are in the majority. Divide England into three parts; two-thirds at least are Catholic at heart, though many conceal their convictions in fear of the Queen. English Catholics are of two sorts—one which makes an open profession regardless of consequences, the other believing at the bottom, but unwilling to risk life or fortune, and so submitting outwardly to the heretic laws, but as eager as the Catholic confessors for redemption from slavery.

'The Queen and her party,' he goes on, 'more fear these secret Catholics than those who wear their colours openly. The latter they can fine, disarm, and make innocuous. The others, being outwardly compliant, cannot be touched, nor can any precaution be taken against their rising when the day of divine vengeance shall arrive.

'The counties specially Catholic are the most warlike, and contain harbours and other conveniences for the landing of an invading army. The north towards the Scotch border has been trained in constant fighting. The Scotch nobles on the other side are Catholic and will lend their help. So will all Wales.

'The inhabitants of the midland and southern provinces, where the taint is deepest, are indolent and cowardly, and do not know what war means.

The towns are more corrupt than the country districts. But the strength of England does not lie, as on the Continent, in towns and cities. The town population are merchants and craftsmen, rarely or never nobles or magnates.

' The nobility, who have the real power, reside with their retinues in castles scattered over the land. The wealthy yeomen are strong and honest, all attached to the ancient faith, and may be counted on when an attempt is made for the restoration of it. The knights and gentry are generally well affected also, and will be well to the front. Many of their sons are being now educated in our seminaries. Some are in exile, but all, whether at home or abroad, will be active on our side.

' Of the great peers, marquises, earls, viscounts, and barons, part are with us, part against us. But the latter sort are new creations, whom the Queen has promoted either for heresy or as her personal lovers, and therefore universally abhorred.

' The premier peer of the old stock is the Earl of Arundel, son and heir of the late Duke of Norfolk, whom she has imprisoned because he tried to escape out of the realm. This earl is entirely Catholic, as well as his brothers and kinsmen ; and they have powerful vassals who are eager to revenge the injury of their lord. The Earl of Northumberland and his brothers are Catholics. They too have family wrongs to repay, their father having been this year murdered in the Tower, and they have placed themselves at my disposal. The Earl of Worcester and his heir hate heresy, and are devoted to us with all their dependents. The Earls of Cumberland and Southampton and Viscount Montague are faithful, and have a large following. Besides these we have many of the barons—Dacre, Morley, Vaux, Windsor, Wharton, Lovelace, Stourton, and others besides. The Earl of Westmoreland, with Lord Paget and Sir Francis Englefield, who reside abroad, have been incredibly earnest in promoting our enterprise. With such support, it is impossible that we can fail. These lords and gentlemen, when they see efficient help coming to them, will certainly rise, and for the following reasons :—

' 1. Because some of the principals among them have given me their promise.

' 2. Because, on hearing that Pope Pius intended to excommunicate and depose the Queen sixteen years ago, many Catholics did rise. They only failed because no support was sent them, and the Pope's sentence had not at that time been actually published. Now, when the Pope has spoken and help is certain, there is not a doubt how they will act.

' 3. Because the Catholics are now much more numerous, and have received daily instruction in their religion from our priests. There is now no orthodox Catholic in the whole realm who supposes that he is any longer bound in conscience to obey the Queen. Books for the occasion have been written and published by us, in which we prove that it is not only lawful for Catholics, but their positive duty, to fight against the Queen and heresy when the Pope bids them; and these books are so greedily read among them that when the time comes they are certain to take arms.

' 4. The Catholics in these late years have shown their real feeling in the martyrdoms of priests and laymen, and in attempts made by several of them against the person and State of the Queen. Various Catholics have tried to kill her at the risk of their own lives, and are still trying.

' 5. We have three hundred priests dispersed among the houses of the nobles and honest gentry. Every day we add to their number; and these priests will direct the consciences and actions of the Catholics at the great crisis.

' 6. They have been so harried and so worried that they hate the heretics worse than they hate the Turks.

' Should any of them fear the introduction of a Spanish army as dangerous to their national liberties, there is an easy way to satisfy their scruples. Let it be openly declared that the enterprise is undertaken in the name of the Pope, and there will be no more hesitation. We have ourselves prepared a book for their instruction, to be issued at the right moment. If his Holiness desires to see it we will have it translated into Latin for his use.

'Before the enterprise is undertaken the sentence of excommunication and deposition ought to be reissued, with special clauses.

'It must be published in all adjoining Catholic countries; all Catholic kings and princes must be admonished to forbid every description of intercourse with the pretended Queen and her heretic subjects, and themselves especially to make or observe no treaties with her, to send no embassies to her and admit none; to render no help to her of any sort or kind.

'Besides those who will be our friends for religion's sake we shall have others with us—neutrals or heretics of milder sort, or atheists, with whom England now abounds, who will join us in the interest of the Queen of Scots. Among them are the Marquis of Winchester, the Earls of Shrewsbury, Derby, Oxford, Rutland, and several other peers. The Queen of Scots herself will be of infinite assistance to us in securing these. She knows who are her secret friends. She has been able so far, and we trust will always be able, to communicate with them. She will see that they are ready at the right time. She has often written to me to say that she hopes that she will be able to escape when the time comes. In her last letter she urges me to be vehement with his Holiness in pushing on the enterprise, and bids him have no

concern for her own safety. She believes that she
can care for herself. If not, she says she will lose
her life willingly in a cause so sacred.

'The enemies that we shall have to deal with
are the more determined heretics whom we call
Puritans, and certain creatures of the Queen, the
Earls of Leicester and Huntingdon, and a few
others. They will have an advantage in the money
in the Treasury, the public arms and stores, and the
army and navy, but none of them have ever seen a
camp. The leaders have been nuzzled in love-
making and Court pleasures, and they will all fly
at the first shock of war. They have not a man
who can command in the field. In the whole
realm there are but two fortresses which could
stand a three days' siege. The people are ener-
vated by long peace, and, except a few who have
served with the heretics in Flanders, cannot bear
their arms. Of those few some are dead and
some have deserted to the Prince of Parma, a
clear proof of the real disposition to revolt. There
is abundance of food and cattle in the country, all
of which will be at our service and cannot be kept
from us. Everywhere there are safe and roomy
harbours, almost all undefended. An invading
force can be landed with ease, and there will be
no lack of local pilots. Fifteen thousand trained
soldiers will be sufficient, aided by the Catholic
English, though, of course, the larger the force,
particularly if it includes cavalry, the quicker the

work will be done and the less the expense.
Practically there will be nothing to overcome save
an unwarlike and undisciplined mob.

' Sixteen times England has been invaded.
Twice only the native race have repelled the
attacking force. They have been defeated on
every other occasion, and with a cause so holy and
just as ours we need not fear to fail. The expenses shall be repaid to his Holiness and the
Catholic King out of the property of the heretics
and the Protestant clergy. There will be ample in
these resources to compensate all who give us their
hand. But the work must be done promptly.
Delay will be infinitely dangerous. If we put off,
as we have done hitherto, the Catholics will be
tired out and reduced in numbers and strength.
The nobles and priests now in exile, and able to be
of such service, will break down in poverty. The
Queen of Scots may be executed or die a natural
death, or something may happen to the Catholic
King or his Holiness. The Queen of England may
herself die, a heretic Government may be recon-
structed under a heretic successor, the young
Scotch king or some other, and our case will then
be desperate ; whereas if we can prevent this and
save the Queen of Scots there will be good hope of
converting her son and reducing the whole island
to the obedience of the faith. Now is the moment.
The French Government cannot interfere. The
Duke of Guise will help us for the sake of the faith

and for his kinswoman.   The Turks are quiet.   The
Church was never stronger or more united.   Part of
Italy is under the Catholic King; the rest is in league
with his Holiness.   The revolt in the Low Countries
is all but crushed.   The sea provinces are on the
point of surrendering.   If they give up the contest
their harbours will be at our service for the invasion.   If not, the way to conquer them is to conquer England.

' I need not urge how much it imports his
Holiness to undertake this glorious work.   He,
supremely wise as he is, knows that from this
Jezebel and her supporters come all the perils
which disturb the Christian world.   He knows
that heretical depravity and all our other miseries
can only end when this woman is chastised.   Reverence for his Holiness and love for my afflicted
country force me to speak.   I submit to his most
holy judgment myself and my advice.'

The most ardent Catholic apologist will hardly
maintain, in the face of this document, that the
English Jesuits and seminary priests were the
innocent missionaries of religion which the modern
enemies of Elizabeth's Government describe them.
Father Parsons, the writer of it, was himself the
leader and director of the Jesuit invasion, and
cannot be supposed to have misrepresented the
purpose for which they had been sent over.   The
point of special interest is the account which he

gives of the state of parties and general feeling in
the English people. Was there that wide disposition to welcome an invading army in so large a
majority of the nation ? The question is supposed
to have been triumphantly answered three years
later, when it is asserted that the difference of
creed was forgotten, and Catholics and Protestants
fought side by side for the liberties of England.
But, in the first place, the circumstances were
changed. The Queen of Scots no longer lived,
and the success of the Armada implied a foreign
sovereign. But, next, the experiment was not tried.
The battle was fought at sea, by a fleet four-fifths
of which was composed of Protestant adventurers,
fitted out and manned by those zealous Puritans
whose fidelity to the Queen Parsons himself admitted. Lord Howard may have been an Anglo-
Catholic ; Roman Catholic he never was ; but he
and his brother were the only loyalists in the House
of Howard. Arundel and the rest of his kindred
were all that Parsons claimed for them. How the
country levies would have behaved had Parma
landed is still uncertain. It is likely that if the
Spanish army had gained a first success, there
might have been some who would have behaved as
Sir William Stanley did. It is observable that
Parsons mentions Leicester and Huntingdon as
the only powerful peers on whom the Queen could
rely, and Leicester, otherwise the unfittest man in
her dominions, she chose to command her land army.

The Duke of Alva and his master Philip, both of them distrusted political priests. Political priests, they said, did not understand the facts of things. Theological enthusiasm made them credulous of what they wished. But Father Parsons's estimate is confirmed in all its parts by the letters of Mendoza, the Spanish ambassador in London. Mendoza was himself a soldier, and his first duty was to learn the real truth. It may be taken as certain that, with the Queen of Scots still alive to succeed to the throne, at the time of the scene in the House of Commons, with which I began this lecture, the great majority of the country party disliked the Reformers, and were looking forward to the accession of a Catholic sovereign, and as a consequence to a religious revolution.

It explains the difficulty of Elizabeth's position and the inconsistency of her political action. Burghley, Walsingham, Mildmay, Knolles, the elder Bacon, were believing Protestants, and would have had her put herself openly at the head of a Protestant European league. They believed that right and justice were on their side, that their side was God's cause, as they called it, and that God would care for it. Elizabeth had no such complete conviction. She disliked dogmatism, Protestant as well as Catholic. She ridiculed Mr. Cecil and his brothers in Christ. She thought, like Erasmus, that the articles of faith, for which men were so eager to kill one another, were subjects which they

knew very little about, and that every man might
think what he would on such matters without
injury to the commonwealth. To become ' head
of the name ' would involve open war with the
Catholic powers. War meant war taxes, which
more than half her subjects would resent and resist.
Religion as she understood it was a development
of law—the law of moral conduct. You could not
have two laws in one country, and you could not
have two religions ; but the outward form mattered
comparatively little. The people she ruled over
were divided about these forms. They were mainly
fools, and if she let them each have chapels and
churches of their own, molehills would become
mountains, and the congregations would go from
arguing into fighting. With Parliament to help
her, therefore, she established a Liturgy, in which
those who wished to find the Mass could hear the
Mass, while those who wanted predestination and
justification by faith could find it in the Articles.
Both could meet under a common roof, and use a
common service, if they would only be reasonable.
If they would not be reasonable, the Catholics
might have their own ritual in their own houses,
and would not be interfered with.

This system continued for the first eleven years
of Elizabeth's reign. No Catholic, she could
proudly say, had ever during that time been
molested for his belief. There was a small fine
for non-attendance at church, but even this was

rarely levied, and by the confession of the Jesuits the Queen's policy was succeeding too well. Sensible men began to see that the differences of religion were not things to quarrel over. Faith was growing languid. The elder generation, who had lived through the Edward and Mary revolutions, were satisfied to be left undisturbed; a new generation was growing up, with new ideas; and so the Church of Rome bestirred itself. Elizabeth was excommunicated. The cycle began of intrigue and conspiracy, assassination plots, and Jesuit invasions. Punishments had to follow, and in spite of herself Elizabeth was driven into what the Catholics could call religious persecution. Religious it was not, for the seminary priests were missionaries of treason. But religious it was made to appear. The English gentleman who wished to remain loyal, without forfeiting his faith, was taught to see that a sovereign under the Papal curse had no longer a claim on his allegiance. If he disobeyed the Pope, he had ceased to be a member of the Church of Christ. The Papal party grew in coherence, while, opposed to them as their purpose came in view, the Protestants, who at first had been inclined to Lutheranism, adopted the deeper and sterner creed of Calvin and Geneva. The memories of the Marian cruelties revived again. They saw themselves threatened with a return to stake and fagot. They closed their ranks and resolved to die rather than submit again to Anti-

christ. They might be inferior in numbers. A
plébiscite in England at that moment would have
sent Burghley and Walsingham to the scaffold.
But the Lord could save by few as well as by
many. Judah had but two tribes out of the
twelve, but the words of the men of Judah were
fiercer than the words of Israel.

One great mistake had been made by Parsons.
He could not estimate what he could not understand. He admitted that the inhabitants of the
towns were mainly heretic—London, Bristol,
Plymouth, and the rest—but he despised them as
merchants, craftsmen, mean persons who had no
heart to fight in them. Nothing is more remarkable
in the history of the sixteenth century than the
effect of Calvinism in levelling distinctions of rank
and in steeling and ennobling the character of
common men. In Scotland, in the Low Countries,
in France, there was the same phenomenon. In
Scotland, the Kirk was the creation of the preachers
and the people, and peasants and workmen dared
to stand in the field against belted knights and
barons, who had trampled on their fathers for
centuries. The artisans of the Low Countries had
for twenty years defied the whole power of Spain.
The Huguenots were not a fifth part of the French
nation, yet defeat could never dishearten them.
Again and again they forced crown and nobles to
make terms with them. It was the same in England.
The allegiance to their feudal leaders dissolved

into a higher obligation to the King of kings, whose
elect they believed themselves to be. Election to
them was not a theological phantasm, but an
enlistment in the army of God. A little flock they
might be, but they were a dangerous people to deal
with, most of all in the towns on the sea. The sea
was the element of the Reformers. The Popes had
no jurisdiction over the winds and waves. Rochelle
was the citadel of the Huguenots. The English
merchants and mariners had wrongs of their own,
perpetually renewed, which fed the bitterness of
their indignation. Touch where they would in
Spanish ports, the inquisitor's hand was on their
ships' crews, and the crews, unless they denied
their faith, were handed over to the stake or the
galleys. The Calvinists are accused of intolerance.
I fancy that even in these humane and enlightened
days we should not be very tolerant if the King of
Dahomey were to burn every European visitor to
his dominions who would not worship Mumbo
Jumbo. The Duke of Alva was not very merciful
to heretics, but he tried to bridle the zeal of the
Holy Office in burning the English seamen. Even
Philip himself remonstrated. It was to no purpose.
The Holy Office said they would think about it, but
concluded to go on. I am not the least surprised
if the English seamen were intolerant. I should be
very much surprised if they had not been. The
Queen could not protect them. They had to protect
themselves as they could, and make Spanish vessels,

when they could catch them, pay for the iniquities of their rulers.

With such a temper rising on both sides, Elizabeth's policy had but a poor chance. She still hoped that the better sense of mankind would keep the doctrinal enthusiasts in order. Elizabeth wished her subjects would be content to live together in unity of spirit, if not in unity of theory, in the bond of peace, not hatred, in righteousness of life, not in orthodoxy preached by stake and gibbet. She was content to wait and to persevere. She refused to declare war. War would tear the world in pieces. She knew her danger. She knew that she was in constant peril of assassination. She knew that if the Protestants were crushed in Scotland, in France, and in the Low Countries, her own turn would follow. To protect insurgents avowedly would be to justify insurrection against herself. But what she would not do openly she would do secretly. What she would not do herself she let her subjects do. Thousands of English volunteers fought in Flanders for the States, and in France for the Huguenots. When the English Treasury was shut to the entreaties of Coligny or William of Orange the London citizens untied their purse-strings. Her friends in Scotland fared ill. They were encouraged by promises which were not observed, because to observe them might bring on war. They committed themselves for her sake. They fell one after another—Murray, Morton,

K

Gowrie—into bloody graves. Others took their places and struggled on. The Scotch Reformation was saved. Scotland was not allowed to open its arms to an invading army to strike England across the Border. But this was held to be their sufficient recompense. They cared for their cause as well as for the English Queen, and they had their reward. If they saved her they saved their own country. She too did not lie on a bed of roses. To prevent open war she was exposing her own life to the assassin. At any moment a pistol-shot or a stab with a dagger might add Elizabeth to the list of victims. She knew it, yet she went on upon her own policy, and faced in her person her own share of the risk. One thing only she did. If she would not defend her friends and her subjects as Queen of England, she left them free to defend themselves. She allowed traitors to be hanged when they were caught at their work. She allowed the merchants to fit out their privateer fleets, to defend at their own cost the shores of England, and to teach the Spaniards to fear their vengeance.

But how long was all this to last? How long were loyal citizens to feel that they were living over a loaded mine—throughout their own country, throughout the Continent, at Rome and at Madrid, at Brussels and at Paris, a legion of conspirators were driving their shafts under the English commonwealth. The Queen might be indifferent to her own danger, but on the Queen's life hung the peace of the whole realm. A stroke of a poniard, a touch of a trigger, and swords would be flying from their scabbards in every county; England would become, like France, one wild scene of anarchy and civil war. No successor had been named. The Queen refused to hear a successor declared. Mary Stuart's hand had been in every plot since she crossed the Border. Twice the House of Commons had petitioned for her execution. Elizabeth would neither touch her life nor allow her hopes of the crown to be taken from her. The Bond of Association was but a remedy of despair, and the Act of Parliament would have passed for little in the tempest which would immediately rise. The agony reached a height when the fatal news came from the Netherlands that there at last assassination had done its work. The Prince of Orange, after many failures, had been finished, and a libel was found in the Palace at Westminster exhorting the ladies of the household to provide a Judith among themselves to rid the world of the English Holofernes.

One part of Elizabeth's subjects, at any rate, were not disposed to sit down in patience under the eternal nightmare. From Spain was to come the army of deliverance for which the Jesuits were so passionately longing. To the Spaniards the Pope was looking for the execution of the Bull of Deposition. Father Parsons had left out of his estimate the Protestant adventurers of London and Plymouth, who, besides their creed and their patriotism, had their private wrongs to revenge. Philip might talk of peace, and perhaps in weariness might at times seriously wish for it ; but between the Englishmen whose life was on the ocean and the Spanish Inquisition, which had burned so many of them, there was no peace possible. To them, Spain was the natural enemy. Among the daring spirits who had sailed with Drake round the globe, who had waylaid the Spanish gold ships, and startled the world with their exploits, the joy of whose lives had been to fight Spaniards wherever they could meet with them, there was but one wish—for an honest open war. The great galleons were to them no objects of terror. The Spanish naval power seemed to them a ' Colossus stuffed with clouts.' They were Protestants all of them, but their theology was rather practical than speculative. If Italians and Spaniards chose to believe in the Mass, it was not any affair of theirs. Their quarrel was with the insolent pretence of Catholics to force their creed on others with sword and cannon. The spirit which was working in them was the genius of freedom. On their own element they felt that they could be the spiritual tyrants' masters. But as things were going, rebellion was likely to break out at home ; their homesteads might be burning, their country overrun with the Prince of Parma's army, the Inquisition at their own doors, and a

Catholic sovereign bringing back the fagots of Smithfield.

The Reformation at its origin was no introduction of novel heresies. It was a revolt of the laity of Europe against the profligacy and avarice of the clergy. The popes and cardinals pretended to be the representatives of Heaven. When called to account for abuse of their powers, they had behaved precisely as mere corrupt human kings and aristocracies behave. They had intrigued; they had excommunicated; they had set nation against nation, sovereigns against their subjects; they had encouraged assassination; they had made themselves infamous by horrid massacres, and had taught one half of foolish Christendom to hate the other. The hearts of the poor English seamen whose comrades had been burnt at Seville to make a Spanish holiday, thrilled with a sacred determination to end such scenes. The purpose that was in them broke into a wild war-music, as the wind harp swells and screams under the breath of the storm. I found in the Record Office an unsigned letter of some inspired old sea-dog, written in a bold round hand and addressed to Elizabeth. The ships' companies which in summer served in Philip's men-of-war went in winter in thousands to catch cod on the Banks of Newfoundland. 'Give me five vessels,' the writer said, 'and I will go out and sink them all, and the galleons shall rot in Cadiz Harbour for want of hands to sail them. But decide, Madam, and decide quickly. Time flies, and will not return. *The wings of man's life are plumed with the feathers of death.'*

The Queen did not decide. The five ships were not sent, and the poor Castilian sailors caught their cod in peace. But in spite of herself Elizabeth was driven forward by the tendencies of things. The death of the Prince of Orange left the States without a Government. The Prince of Parma was pressing them hard. Without a leader they were lost. They offered themselves to Elizabeth, to be incorporated in the English Empire. They said that if she refused they must either submit to Spain or become provinces of France. The Netherlands, whether Spanish or French, would be equally dangerous to England. The Netherlands once brought back under the Pope, England's turn would come next ; while to accept the proposal meant instant and desperate war, both with France and Spain too—for France would never allow England again to gain a foot on the Continent. Elizabeth knew not what to do. She would and she would not. She did not accept ; she did not refuse. It was neither No nor Yes. Philip, who was as fond of indirect ways as herself, proposed to quicken her irresolution.

The harvest had failed in Galicia, and the population were starving. England grew more corn than she wanted, and, under a special promise that the crews should not be molested, a fleet of corn-traders had gone with cargoes of grain to Coruña, Bilbao, and Santander. The King of Spain, on hearing that Elizabeth was treating with the States, issued a sudden order to seize the vessels, confiscate the cargoes, and imprison the men. The order was executed. One English ship only was lucky enough to escape by the adroitness of her commander. The *Primrose*, of London, lay in Bilbao Roads with a captain and fifteen hands. The mayor, on receiving the order, came on board to look over the ship. He then went on shore for a sufficient force to carry out the seizure. After he was gone the captain heard of the fate which was intended for him. The mayor returned with two boatloads of soldiers, stepped up the ladder, touched the captain on the shoulder, and told him he was a prisoner. The Englishmen snatched pike and cutlass, pistol and battleaxe, killed seven or eight of the Spanish boarders, threw the rest overboard, and flung stones on them as they scrambled into their boats. The mayor, who had fallen into the sea, caught a rope and was hauled up when the fight was over. The cable was cut, the sails hoisted, and in a few minutes the *Primrose* was under way for England, with the mayor of Bilbao below the hatches. No second vessel got away. If Philip had meant to frighten Elizabeth he could not have taken a worse means of doing it, for he had exasperated that particular part of the English population which was least afraid of him. He had broken faith besides, and had seized some hundreds of merchants and sailors who had gone merely to relieve Spanish distress. Elizabeth, as usual, would not act herself. She sent no ships from her own navy to demand reparation; but she gave the adventurers a free hand. The London and Plymouth citizens determined to read Spain a lesson which should make an impression. They had the worst fears for the fate of the prisoners ; but if they could not save, they could avenge them. Sir Francis Drake, who wished for nothing better than to be at work again, volunteered his services, and a fleet was collected at Plymouth of twenty-five sail, every one of them fitted out by private enterprise. No finer armament, certainly no better-equipped armament, ever left the English shores. The expenses were, of course, enormous. Of seamen and soldiers there were between two and three thousand. Drake's name was worth an army. The cost was to be recovered out of the expedition somehow ; the Spaniards were to be made to pay for it; but how or when was left to Drake's judgment. This time there was no second in command sent by the friends of Spain to hang upon his arm. By universal consent he had the absolute command. His instructions were merely to inquire at Spanish ports into the meaning of the arrest. Beyond that he was left to go where he pleased and do what he pleased on his own responsibility. The Queen said frankly that if it proved convenient she intended to disown him. Drake had no objection to being disowned, so he could teach the Spaniards to be more careful how they handled Englishmen. What came of it will be the subject of the next lecture. Father Parsons said the Protestant traders of England had grown effeminate and dared not fight. In the ashes of their own smoking cities the Spaniards had to learn that Father Parsons had misread his countrymen. If Drake had been given to heroics he might have left Virgil's lines inscribed above the broken arms of Castile at St. Domingo :

> En ego victa situ quam veri effeta senectus
> Arma inter regum falsa formidine ludit :
> Respice ad hæc.

LECTURE VI

THE GREAT EXPEDITION TO THE WEST INDIES

QUEEN ELIZABETH and her brother-in-law of Spain were reluctant champions of opposing principles In themselves they had no wish to quarrel, but each was driven forward by fate and circumstance —Philip by the genius of the Catholic religion, Elizabeth by the enthusiasts for freedom and by the advice of statesmen who saw no safety for her except in daring. Both wished for peace, and refused to see that peace was impossible ; but both were compelled to yield to their subjects' eagerness. Philip had to threaten England with invasion ; Elizabeth had to show Philip that England had a long arm, which Spanish wisdom would do well to fear. It was a singular position. Philip had outraged orthodoxy and dared the anger of Rome by maintaining an ambassador at Elizabeth's Court after her excommunication. He had laboured for a reconciliation with a sincerity which his secret letters make it impossible to doubt. He had condescended even to sue for it, in spite of Drake and the voyage of the *Pelican* ; yet he had helped the Pope to set Ireland in a flame. He had encouraged Elizabeth's Catholic subjects in conspiracy after conspiracy. He had approved of attempts to dispose of her as he had disposed of the Prince of Orange. Elizabeth had retaliated, though with half a heart, by letting her soldiers volunteer into the service of the revolted Netherlands, by permitting English privateers to plunder the Spanish colonies, seize the gold ships, and revenge their own wrongs. Each, perhaps, had wished to show the other what an open war would cost them both, and each drew back when war appeared inevitable.

Events went their way. Holland and Zeeland, driven to extremity, had petitioned for incorporation with England; as a counter-stroke and a warning, Philip had arrested the English corn ships and imprisoned the owners and the crews. Her own fleet was nothing. The safety of the English shores depended on the spirit of the adventurers, and she could not afford to check the anger with which the news was received. To accept the offer of the States was war, and war she would not have. Herself, she would not act at all; but in her usual way she might let her subjects act for themselves, and plead, as Philip pleaded in excuse for the Inquisition, that she could not restrain them. And thus it was that in September 1585, Sir Francis Drake found himself with a fleet of twenty-five privateers and 2,500 men who had volunteered to serve with him under his own command. He had no distinct commission. The expedition had been fitted out as a private undertaking. Neither officers nor crews had been engaged for the service of the Crown. They received no wages. In the eye of the law they were pirates. They were going on their own account to read the King of Spain a necessary lesson and pay their expenses at the King of Spain's cost. Young Protestant England had taken fire. The name of Drake set every Protestant heart burning, and hundreds of gallant gentlemen had pressed in to join. A grandson of Burghley had come, and Edward Winter the Admiral's son, and Francis Knolles the Queen's cousin, and Martin Frobisher, and Christopher Carlile. Philip Sidney had wished to make one also in the glory; but Philip Sidney was needed elsewhere. The Queen's consent had been won from her at a bold interval in her shifting moods. The hot fit might pass away, and Burghley sent Drake a hint to be off before her humour changed. No word was said. On the morning of the 14th of September the signal flag was flying from Drake's maintop to up anchor and away. Drake, as he admitted after, ' was not the most assured of her Majesty's perseverance to let them go forward.' Past Ushant he would be beyond reach of recall. With light winds and calms they drifted across the Bay. They fell in with a few Frenchmen homeward-bound from the Banks, and let them pass uninjured. A large Spanish ship which they met next day, loaded with excellent fresh salt fish, was counted lawful prize.

The fish was new and good, and was distributed through the fleet. Standing leisurely on, they cleared Finisterre and came up with the Isles of Bayona, at the mouth of Vigo Harbour. They dropped anchor there, and ' it was a great matter and a royal sight to see them.' The Spanish Governor, Don Pedro Bemadero, sent off with some astonishment to know who and what they were. Drake answered with a question whether England and Spain were at war, and if not why the English merchants had been arrested. Don Pedro could but say that he knew of no war, and for the merchants an order had come for their release. For reply Drake landed part of his force on the islands, and Don Pedro, not knowing what to make of such visitors, found it best to propitiate them with cartloads of wine and fruit. The weather, which had been hitherto fine, showed signs of change. The wind rose, and the sea with it. The anchorage was exposed, and Drake sent Christopher Carlile with one of his ships and a few pinnaces, up the harbour to look out for better shelter. Their appearance created a panic in the town. The alarmed inhabitants took to their boats, carrying off their property and their Church plate. Carlile, who had a Calvinistic objection to idolatry, took the liberty of detaining part of these treasures. From one boat he took a massive silver cross belonging to the High Church at Vigo ; from another an image of Our Lady, which the sailors relieved of her clothes and were

said, when she was stripped, to have treated with
some indignity. Carlile's report being satisfactory,
the whole fleet was brought the next day up the
harbour and moored above the town. The news
had by this time spread into the country. The
Governor of Galicia came down with all the force
which he could collect in a hurry. Perhaps he was
in time to save Vigo itself. Perhaps Drake, having
other aims in view, did not care to be detained
over a smaller object. The Governor, at any rate,
saw that the English were too strong for him to
meddle with. The best that he could look for was
to persuade them to go away on the easiest terms.
Drake and he met in boats for a parley. Drake
wanted water and fresh provisions. Drake was to
be allowed to furnish himself undisturbed. He had
secured what he most wanted. He had shown the
King of Spain that he was not invulnerable in his
own home dominion, and he sailed away unmolested.
Madrid was in consternation. That the English
could dare insult the first prince in Europe on the
sacred soil of the Peninsula itself seemed like a
dream. The Council of State sat for three days
considering the meaning of it. Drake's name was
already familiar in Spanish ears. It was not con-
ceivable that he had come only to inquire after the
arrested ships and seamen. But what could the
English Queen be about ? Did she not know that she
existed only by the forbearance of Philip ? Did she
know the King of Spain's force ? Did not she and

her people quake? Little England, it was said by some of these councillors, was to be swallowed at a mouthful by the King of half the world. The old Admiral Santa Cruz was less confident about the swallowing. He observed that England had many teeth, and that instead of boasting of Spanish greatness it would be better to provide against what she might do with them. Till now the corsairs had appeared only in twos and threes. With such a fleet behind him Drake might go where he pleased. He might be going to the South Seas again. He might take Madeira if he liked, or the Canary Islands. Santa Cruz himself thought he would make for the West Indies and Panama, and advised the sending out there instantly every available ship that they had.

The gold fleet was Drake's real object. He had information that it would be on its way to Spain by the Cape de Verde Islands, and he had learnt the time when it was to be expected. From Vigo he sailed for the Canaries, looked in at Palma, with 'intention to have taken our pleasure there,' but found the landing dangerous and the town itself not worth the risk. He ran on to the Cape de Verde Islands. He had measured his time too narrowly. The gold fleet had arrived and had gone. He had missed it by twelve hours, 'the reason,' as he said with a sigh, 'best known to God.' The chance of prize money was lost, but the political purpose of the expedition could still be completed. The Cape de Verde Islands could not sail away, and a begin-

ning could be made with Sant Iago. Sant Iago
was a thriving, well-populated town, and down in
Drake's book as specially needing notice, some
Plymouth sailors having been recently murdered
there. Christopher Carlile, always handy and
trustworthy, was put on shore with a thousand
men to attack the place on the undefended side.
The Spanish commander, the bishop, and most of
the people fled, as at Vigo, into the mountains
with their plate and money. Carlile entered without opposition, and flew St. George's Cross from
the castle as a signal to the fleet. Drake came in,
landed the rest of his force, and took possession.
It happened to be the 17th of November—the anni-
versary of the Queen's accession—and ships and
batteries, dressed out with English flags, celebrated
the occasion with salvoes of cannon. Houses and
magazines were then searched and plundered.
Wine was found in large quantities, rich mer-
chandise for the Indian trade, and other valuables.
Of gold and silver nothing—it had all been removed. Drake waited for a fortnight, hoping that
the Spaniards would treat for the ransom of the
city. When they made no sign, he marched twelve
miles inland to a village where the Governor and
the Bishop were said to have taken refuge. But
the village was found deserted. The Spaniards
had gone to the mountains, where it was useless
to follow them, and were too proud to bargain with
a pirate chief. Sant Iago was a beautifully built

city, and Drake would perhaps have spared it ; but a ship-boy who had strayed was found murdered and barbarously mutilated. The order was given to burn. Houses, magazines, churches, public buildings were turned to ashes, and the work being finished Drake went on, as Santa Cruz expected, for the Spanish West Indies. The Spaniards were magnificent in all that they did and touched. They built their cities in their new possessions on the most splendid models of the Old World. St. Domingo and Carthagena had their castles and cathedrals, palaces, squares, and streets, grand and solid as those at Cadiz and Seville, and raised as enduring monuments of the power and greatness of the Castilian monarchs. To these Drake meant to pay a visit. Beyond them was the Isthmus, where he had made his first fame and fortune, with Panama behind, the depôt of the Indian treasure. So far all had gone well with him. He had taken what he wanted out of Vigo ; he had destroyed Sant Iago and had not lost a man. Unfortunately he had now a worse enemy to deal with than Spanish galleons or Spanish garrisons. He was in the heat of the tropics. Yellow fever broke out and spread through the fleet. Of those who caught the infection few recovered, or recovered only to be the wrecks of themselves. It was swift in its work. In a few days more than two hundred had died. But the north-east trade blew merrily. The fleet sped on before it. In eighteen days they

L

were in the roads at Dominica, the island of brooks and rivers and fruit. Limes and lemons and oranges were not as yet. But there were leaves and roots of the natural growth, known to the Caribs as antidotes to the fever, and the Caribs, when they learnt that the English were the Spaniards' enemies, brought them this precious remedy and taught them the use of it. The ships were washed and ventilated, and the water casks refilled. The infection seemed to have gone as suddenly as it appeared, and again all was well.

Christmas was kept at St. Kitts, which was then uninhabited. A council of war was held to consider what should be done next. St. Domingo lay nearest to them. It was the finest of all the Spanish colonial cities. It was the capital of the West Indian Government, the great centre of West Indian commerce. In the cathedral, before the high altar, lay Columbus and his brother Diego. In natural wealth no island in the world outrivals Espinola, where the city stood. A vast population had collected there, far away from harm, protected as they supposed, by the majesty of the mother country, the native inhabitants almost exterminated, themselves undreaming that any enemy could approach them from the ocean, and therefore negligent of defence and enjoying themselves in easy security.

Drake was to give them a new experience and a lesson for the future. On their way across from

St. Kitts the adventurers overhauled a small vessel bound to the same port as they were. From the crew of this vessel they learnt that the harbour at St. Domingo was formed, like so many others in the West Indies, by a long sandspit, acting as a natural breakwater. The entrance was a narrow inlet at the extremity of the spit, and batteries had been mounted there to cover it. To land on the outer side of the sandbank was made impossible by the surf. There was one sheltered point only where boats could go on shore, but this was ten miles distant from the town.

Ten miles was but a morning's march. Drake went in himself in a pinnace, surveyed the landing-place, and satisfied himself of its safety. The plan of attack at Sant Iago was to be exactly repeated. On New Year's Eve Christopher Carlile was again landed with half the force in the fleet. Drake remained with the rest, and prepared to force the entrance of the harbour if Carlile succeeded. Their coming had been seen from the city. The alarm had been given, and the women and children, the money in the treasury, the consecrated plate, movable property of all kinds, were sent off inland as a precaution. Of regular troops there seem to have been none, but in so populous a city there was no difficulty in collecting a respectable force to defend it. The hidalgos formed a body of cavalry. The people generally were unused to arms, but they were Spaniards and brave men, and did not mean

to leave their homes without a fight for it.   Carlile
lay still for the night.   He marched at eight in the
morning on New Year's Day, advanced leisurely,
and at noon found himself in front of the wall.   So
far he had met no resistance, but a considerable
body of horse—gentlemen and their servants chiefly
—charged down on him out of the bush and out of
the town.   He formed into a square to receive
them.   They came on gallantly, but were received
with pike and shot, and after a few attempts gave
up and retired.   Two gates were in front of Carlile,
with a road to each leading through a jungle.
At each gate were cannon, and the jungle was lined
with musketeers.   He divided his men and attacked
both together.   One party he led in person.   The
cannon opened on him, and an Englishman next
to him was killed.   He dashed on, leaving the
Spaniards no time to reload, carried the gate at a
rush, and cut his way through the streets to the
great square.   The second division had been
equally successful, and St. Domingo was theirs
except the castle, which was still untaken.   Carlile's
numbers were too small to occupy a large city.   He
threw up barricades and fortified himself in the
square for the night.   Drake brought the fleet in at
daybreak, and landed guns, when the castle surrendered.   A messenger—a negro boy—was sent
to the governor to learn the terms which he was
prepared to offer to save the city from pillage.   The
Spanish officers were smarting with the disgrace.

One of them struck the lad through the body with a lance. He ran back bleeding to the English lines and died at Drake's feet. Sir Francis was a dangerous man to provoke. Such doings had to be promptly stopped. In the part of the town which he occupied was a monastery with a number of friars in it. The religious orders, he well knew, were the chief instigators of the policy which was maddening the world. He sent two of these friars with the provost-marshal to the spot where the boy had been struck, promptly hanged them, and then despatched another to tell the governor that he would hang two more every day at the same place till the officer was punished. The Spaniards had long learnt to call Drake the Draque, the serpent, the devil. They feared that the devil might be a man of his word. The offender was surrendered. It was not enough. Drake insisted that they should do justice on him themselves. The governor found it prudent to comply, and the too hasty officer was executed.

The next point was the ransom of the city. The Spaniards still hesitating, 200 men were told off each morning to burn, while the rest searched the private houses, and palaces, and magazines. Government House was the grandest building in the New World. It was approached by broad flights of marble stairs. Great doors opened on a spacious gallery leading into a great hall, and above the portico hung the arms of Spain—a globe representing the world, a horse leaping upon it, and in the horse's mouth a scroll with the haughty motto, ' Non sufficit orbis.' Palace and scutcheon were levelled into dust by axe and gunpowder, and each day for a month the destruction went on, Drake's demands steadily growing and the unhappy governor vainly pleading impossibility.

Vandalism, atrocity unheard of among civilised nations, dishonour to the Protestant cause, Drake deserving to swing at his own yardarm ; so indignant Liberalism shrieked, and has not ceased shrieking. Let it be remembered that for fifteen years the Spaniards had been burning English seamen whenever they could catch them, plotting to kill the Queen and reduce England itself into vassaldom to the Pope. The English nation, the loyal part of it, were replying to the wild pretension by the hands of their own admiral. If Philip chose to countenance assassins, if the Holy Office chose to burn English sailors as heretics, those heretics had a right to make Spain understand that such a game was dangerous, that, as Santa Cruz had said, they had teeth and could use them.

It was found in the end that the governor's plea of impossibility was more real than was at first believed. The gold and silver had been really carried off. All else that was valuable had been burnt or taken by the English. The destruction of a city so solidly built was tedious and difficult. Nearly half of it was blown up. The cathedral was spared, perhaps as the resting-place of Columbus. Drake had other work before him. After staying a month in undisturbed occupation he agreed to accept 25,000 ducats as a ransom for what was left and sailed away.

It was now February. The hot season was coming on, when the climate would be dangerous. There was still much to do and the time was running short. Panama had to be left for another opportunity. Drake's object was to deal blows which would shake the faith of Europe in the Spanish power. Carthagena stood next to St. Domingo among the Spanish West Indian fortresses. The situation was strong. In 1740 Carthagena was able to beat off Vernon and a great English fleet. But Drake's crews were in high health and spirits, and he determined to see what he could do with it. Surprise was no longer to be hoped for. The alarm had spread over the Caribbean Sea. But in their present humour they were ready to go anywhere and dare anything, and to Carthagena they went.

Drake's name carried terror before it. Every non-combatant—old men, women and children—had been cleared out before he arrived, but the rest prepared for a smart defence. The harbour at Carthagena was formed, as at St. Domingo and Port Royal, by a sandspit. The spit was long, narrow, in places not fifty yards wide, and covered with prickly bush, and along this, as before, it was

necessary to advance to reach the city. A trench
had been cut across at the neck, and a stiff barri-
cade built and armed with heavy guns; behind
this were several hundred musketeers, while the
bush was full of Indians with poisoned arrows.
Pointed stakes—poisoned also—had been driven
into the ground along the approaches, on which to
step was death. Two large galleys, full of men,
patrolled inside the bank on the harbour edge, and
with these preparations the inhabitants hoped to
keep the dreadful Drake from reaching them.
Carlile, as before, was to do the land fighting. He
was set on shore three miles down the spit. The
tide is slight in those seas, but he waited till it was
out, and advanced along the outer shore at low-
water mark. He was thus covered by the bank
from the harbour galleys, and their shots passed
over him. Two squadrons of horse came out, but
could do nothing to him on the broken ground.
The English pushed on to the wall, scarcely losing
a man. They charged, scaled the parapets, and
drove the Spanish infantry back at point of pike.
Carlile killed their commander with his own hand.
The rest fled after a short struggle, and Drake was
master of Carthagena. Here for six weeks he
remained. The Spaniards withdrew out of the
city, and there were again parleys over the ransom
money. Courtesies were exchanged among the
officers. Drake entertained the governor and
his suite. The governor returned the hospitality

and received Drake and the English captains. Drake demanded 100,000 ducats. The Spaniards offered 30,000, and protested that they could pay no more. The dispute might have lasted longer, but it was cut short by the reappearance of the yellow fever in the fleet, this time in a deadlier form. The Spanish offer was accepted, and Carthagena was left to its owners. It was time to be off, for the heat was telling, and the men began to drop with appalling rapidity. Nombre de Dios and Panama were near and under their lee, and Drake threw longing eyes on what, if all else had been well, might have proved an easy capture. But on a review of their strength, it was found that there were but 700 fit for duty who could be spared for the service, and a council of war decided that a march across the Isthmus with so small a force was too dangerous to be ventured. Enough had been done for glory, enough for the political impression to be made in Europe. The King of Spain had been dared in his own dominions. Three fine Spanish cities had been captured by storm and held to ransom. In other aspects the success had fallen short of expectation. This time they had taken no *Cacafuego* with a year's produce of the mines in her hold. The plate and coin had been carried off, and the spoils had been in a form not easily turned to value. The expedition had been fitted out by private persons to pay its own cost. The result in money was but 60,000*l*. Forty

thousand had to be set aside for expenses. There
remained but 20,000*l.* to be shared among the
ships' companies. Men and officers had entered,
high and low, without wages, on the chance of
what they might get. The officers and owners
gave a significant demonstration of the splendid
spirit in which they had gone about their work.
They decided to relinquish their own claims on the
ransom paid for Carthagena, and bestow the same
on the common seamen, 'wishing it were so much
again as would be a sufficient reward for their
painful endeavour.'

Thus all were well satisfied, conscious all that
they had done their duty to their Queen and
country. The adventurers' fleet turned homewards
at the beginning of April. What men could do
they had achieved. They could not fight against
the pestilence of the tropics. For many days the
yellow fever did its deadly work among them, and
only slowly abated. They were delayed by calms
and unfavourable winds. Their water ran short.
They had to land again at Cape Antonio, the
western point of Cuba, and sink wells to supply
themselves. Drake himself, it was observed,
worked with spade and bucket, like the meanest
person in the whole company, always foremost
where toil was to be endured or honour won, the
wisest in the devising of enterprises, the calmest in
danger, the first to set an example of energy in
difficulties, and, above all, the firmest in maintain-

ing order and discipline. The fever slackened as they reached the cooler latitudes. They worked their way up the Bahama Channel, going north to avoid the trades. The French Protestants had been attempting to colonise in Florida. The Spaniards had built a fortress on the coast, to observe their settlements and, as occasion offered, cut Huguenot throats. As he passed by Drake paid this fortress a visit and wiped it out. Farther north again he was in time to save the remnant of an English settlement, rashly planted there by another brilliant servant of Queen Elizabeth.

Of all the famous Elizabethans Sir Walter Raleigh is the most romantically interesting. His splendid and varied gifts, his chequered fortunes, and his cruel end, will embalm his memory in English history. But Raleigh's great accomplishments promised more than they performed. His hand was in everything, but of work successfully completed he had less to show than others far his inferiors, to whom fortune had offered fewer opportunities. He was engaged in a hundred schemes at once, and in every one of them there was always some taint of self, some personal ambition or private object to be gained. His life is a record of undertakings begun in enthusiasm, maintained imperfectly, and failures in the end. Among his other adventures he had sent a colony to Virginia. He had imagined, or had been led by others to believe, that there was an Indian Court there brilliant as

Montezuma's, an enlightened nation crying to be admitted within the charmed circle of Gloriana's subjects. His princes and princesses proved things of air, or mere Indian savages; and of Raleigh there remains nothing in Virginia save the name of the city which is called after him. The starving survivors of his settlement on the Roanoke River were taken on board by Drake's returning squadron and carried home to England, where they all arrived safely, to the glory of God, as our pious ancestors said and meant in unconventional sincerity, on the 28th of July, 1586.

The expedition, as I have said, barely paid its cost. In the shape of wages the officers received nothing, and the crews but a few pounds a man; but there was, perhaps, not one of them who was not better pleased with the honour which he had brought back than if he had come home loaded with doubloons.

Startled Catholic Europe meanwhile rubbed its eyes and began to see that the 'enterprise of England,' as the intended invasion was called, might not be the easy thing which the seminary priests described it. The seminary priests had said that so far as England was Protestant at all it was Protestant only by the accident of its Government, that the immense majority of the people were Catholic at heart and were thirsting for a return to the fold, that on the first appearance of a Spanish army of deliverance the whole edifice

which Elizabeth had raised would crumble to the
ground. I suppose it is true that if the world had
then been advanced to its present point of progress,
if there had been then recognised a Divine right to
rule in the numerical majority, even without a
Spanish army the seminary priests would have
had their way. Elizabeth's Parliaments were con-
trolled by the municipalities of the towns, and the
towns were Protestant. A Parliament chosen by
universal suffrage and electoral districts would have
sent Cecil and Walsingham into private life or to
the scaffold, replaced the Mass in the churches, and
reduced the Queen, if she had been left on the
throne, into the humble servant of the Pope and
Philip. It would not perhaps have lasted, but
that, so far as I can judge, would have been the
immediate result, and instead of a Reformation we
should have had the light come in the shape of
lightning. But I have often asked my Radical
friends what is to be done if out of every hundred
enlightened voters two-thirds will give their votes
one way, but are afraid to fight, and the remaining
third will not only vote but will fight too if the poll
goes against them. Which has then the right to
rule ? I can tell them which will rule. The brave
and resolute minority will rule. Plato says that if
one man was stronger than all the rest of mankind
he would rule all the rest of mankind. It must be
so, because there is no appeal. The majority must
be prepared to assert their Divine right with their

right hands, or it will go the way that other Divine
rights have gone before. I will not believe the
world to have been so ill-constructed that there are
rights which cannot be enforced. It appears to me
that the true right to rule in any nation lies with
those who are best and bravest, whether their
numbers are large or small ; and three centuries
ago the best and bravest part of this English nation
had determined, though they were but a third of
it, that Pope and Spaniard should be no masters of
theirs. Imagination goes for much in such excited
times. To the imagination of Europe in the
sixteenth century the power of Spain appeared
irresistible if she chose to exert it. Heretic Dutchmen might rebel in a remote province, English
pirates might take liberties with Spanish traders,
but the Prince of Parma was making the Dutchmen
feel their master at last. The pirates were but so
many wasps, with venom in their stings, but
powerless to affect the general tendencies of things.
Except to the shrewder eyes of such men as Santa
Cruz the strength of the English at sea had been
left out of count in the calculations of the resources
of Elizabeth's Government. Suddenly a fleet of
these same pirates, sent out, unassisted by their
sovereign, by the private impulse of a few individuals, had insulted the sacred soil of Spain
herself, sailed into Vigo, pillaged the churches,
taken anything that they required, and had gone
away unmolested. They had attacked, stormed,

burnt, or held to ransom three of Spain's proudest colonial cities, and had come home unfought with. The Catholic conspirators had to recognise that they had a worse enemy to deal with than Puritan controversialists or spoilt Court favourites. The Protestant English mariners stood between them and their prey, and had to be encountered on an element which did not bow to popes or princes, before Mary Stuart was to wear Elizabeth's crown or Cardinal Allen be enthroned at Canterbury. It was a revelation to all parties. Elizabeth herself had not expected—perhaps had not wished—so signal a success. War was now looked on as inevitable. The Spanish admirals represented that the national honour required revenge for an injury so open and so insolent. The Pope, who had been long goading the lethargic Philip into action, believed that now at last he would be compelled to move; and even Philip himself, enduring as he was, had been roused to perceive that intrigues and conspiracies would serve his turn no longer. He must put out his strength in earnest, or his own Spaniards might turn upon him as unworthy of the crown of Isabella. Very reluctantly he allowed the truth to be brought home to him. He had never liked the thought of invading England. If he conquered it, he would not be allowed to keep it. Mary Stuart would have to be made queen, and Mary Stuart was part French, and might be wholly French. The burden of the work would be thrown entirely on his shoulders, and his own reward was to be the Church's blessing and the approval of his own conscience—nothing else, so far as he could see. The Pope would recover his annates, his Peter's pence, and his indulgence market.

If the thing was to be done, the Pope, it was clear, ought to pay part of the cost, and this was what the Pope did not intend to do if he could help it. The Pope was flattering himself that Drake's performance would compel Spain to go to war with England whether he assisted or did not. In this matter Philip attempted to undeceive his Holiness. He instructed Olivarez, his ambassador at Rome, to tell the Pope that nothing had been yet done to him by the English which he could not overlook, and unless the Pope would come down with a handsome contribution peace he would make. The Pope stormed and raged; he said he doubted whether Philip was a true son of the Church at all; he flung plates and dishes at the servants' heads at dinner. He said that if he gave Philip money Philip would put it in his pocket and laugh at him. Not one maravedi would he give till a Spanish army was actually landed on English shores, and from this resolution he was not to be moved.

To Philip it was painfully certain that if he invaded and conquered England the English Catholics would insist that he must make Mary Stuart queen He did not like Mary Stuart. He disapproved of her character. He distrusted her promises. Spite of Jesuits and seminary priests, he believed that she was still a Frenchwoman at heart, and a bad woman besides. Yet something he must do for the outraged honour of Castile. He concluded, in his slow way, that he would collect a fleet, the largest and best-appointed that had ever floated on the sea. He would send or lead it in person to the English Channel. He would command the situation with an overwhelming force, and then would choose some course which would be more convenient to himself than to his Holiness at Rome. On the whole he was inclined to let Elizabeth continue queen, and forget and forgive if she would put away her Walsinghams and her Drakes, and would promise to be good for the future. If she remained obstinate his great fleet would cover the passage of the Prince of Parma's army, and he would then dictate his own terms in London.

M

LECTURE VII

ATTACK ON CADIZ

I RECOLLECT being told when a boy, on sending in a bad translation of Horace, that I ought to remember that Horace was a man of intelligence and did not write nonsense. The same caution should be borne in mind by students of history. They see certain things done by kings and statesmen which they believe they can interpret by assuming such persons to have been knaves or idiots. Once an explanation given from the baser side of human nature, they assume that it is necessarily the right one, and they make their Horace into a fool without a misgiving that the folly may lie elsewhere. Remarkable men and women have usually had some rational motive for their conduct, which may be discovered, if we look for it with our eyes open.

Nobody has suffered more from bad translators than Elizabeth. The circumstances of Queen Elizabeth's birth, the traditions of her father, the interests of England, and the sentiments of the party who had sustained her claim to the succession, obliged her on coming to the throne to renew the

separation from the Papacy. The Church of England was re-established on an Anglo-Catholic basis,
which the rival factions might interpret each in
their own way. To allow more than one form of
public worship would have led in the heated temper
of men's minds to quarrels and civil wars. But conscience might be left free under outward conformity,
and those whom the Liturgy did not suit might
use their own ritual in their private houses.
Elizabeth and her wise advisers believed that if
her subjects could be kept from fighting and killing one another, and were not exasperated by outward displays of difference, they would learn that
righteousness of life was more important than
orthodoxy, and to estimate at their real value the
rival dogmas of theology. Had time permitted
the experiment to have a fair trial, it would perhaps have succeeded, but, unhappily for the Queen
and for England, the fire of controversy was still
too hot under the ashes. Protestants and Catholics
had been taught to look on one another as enemies
of God, and were still reluctant to take each other's
hands at the bidding of an Act of Parliament. The
more moderate of the Catholic laity saw no difference so great between the English service and the
Mass as to force them to desert the churches where
their fathers had worshipped for centuries. They
petitioned the Council of Trent for permission to
use the English Prayer Book ; and had the Council
consented, religious dissension would have dissolved

M 2

at last into an innocent difference of opinion. But the Council and the Pope had determined that there should be no compromise with heresy, and the request was refused, though it was backed by Philip's ambassador in London. The action of the Papacy obliged the Queen to leave the Administration in the hands of Protestants, on whose loyalty she could rely. As the struggle with the Reformation spread and deepened she was compelled to assist indirectly the Protestant party in France and Scotland. But she still adhered to her own principle ; she refused to put herself at the head of a Protestant League. She took no step without keeping open a line of retreat on a contrary policy. She had Catholics in her Privy Council who were pensioners of Spain. She filled her household with Catholics, and many a time drove Burghley distracted by listening to them at critical moments. Her constant effort was to disarm the antagonism of the adherents of the old belief, by admitting them to her confidence, and showing them that one part of her subjects was as dear to her as another.

For ten years she went on struggling. For ten years she was proudly able to say that during all that time no Catholic had suffered for his belief either in purse or person. The advanced section of the Catholic clergy was in despair. They saw the consciences of their flocks benumbed and their faith growing lukewarm. They stirred up the

rebellion of the North. They persuaded Pius V.
to force them to a sense of their duties by declaring
Elizabeth excommunicated. They sent their missionaries through the English counties to recover
sheep that were straying, and teach the sin of submission to a sovereign whom the Pope had deposed.
Then had followed the Ridolfi plot, deliberately
encouraged by the Pope and Spain, which had
compelled the Government to tighten the reins.
One conspiracy had followed another. Any means
were held legitimate to rid the world of an enemy
of God. The Queen's character was murdered by
the foulest slanders, and a hundred daggers were
sharpened to murder her person. The King of
Spain had not advised the excommunication,
because he knew that he would be expected to
execute it, and he had other things to do. When
called on to act, he and Alva said that if the
English Catholics wanted Spanish help they must
do something for themselves. To do the priests
justice, they were brave enough. What they did,
and how far they had succeeded in making the
country disaffected, Father Parsons has told you
in the paper which I read to you in a former
lecture. Elizabeth refused to take care of herself.
She would show no distrust. She would not dismiss
the Catholic ladies and gentlemen from the household. She would allow no penal laws to be enforced
against Catholics as such. Repeated conspiracies
to assassinate her were detected and exposed, but

she would take no warning. She would have no
bodyguard. The utmost that she would do was to
allow the Jesuits and seminary priests, who, by
Parsons's own acknowledgment were sowing rebellion, to be banished the realm, and if they persisted
in remaining afterwards, to be treated as traitors.
When executions are treated as martyrdoms, candi-
dates will never be wanting for the crown of glory,
and the flame only burnt the hotter. Tyburn and
the quartering knife was a horrid business, and
Elizabeth sickened over it. She hated the severity
which she was compelled to exercise. Her name
was defiled with the grossest calumnies. She knew
that she might be murdered any day. For herself
she was proudly indifferent; but her death would
and must be followed by a furious civil war. She
told the Privy Council one day after some stormy
scene, that she would come back afterwards and
amuse herself with seeing the Queen of Scots
making their heads fly.

Philip was weary of it too. He had enough to
do in ruling his own dominions without quarrelling
for ever with his sister-in-law. He had seen that
she had subjects, few or many, who, if he struck,
would strike back again. English money and
English volunteers were keeping alive the war in
the Netherlands. English privateers had plundered
his gold ships, destroyed his commerce, and burnt
his West Indian cities—all this in the interests of
the Pope, who gave him fine words in plenty, but

who, when called on for money to help in the
English conquest, only flung about his dinner
plates. The Duke of Alva, while he was alive, and
the Prince of Parma, who commanded in the
Netherlands in Alva's place, advised peace if peace
could be had on reasonable terms. If Elizabeth
would consent to withdraw her help from the
Netherlands, and would allow the English Catholics
the tacit toleration with which her reign had begun,
they were of opinion, and Philip was of opinion too,
that it would be better to forgive Drake and St.
Domingo, abandon Mary Stuart and the seminary
priests, and meddle no more with English internal
politics.

Tired with a condition which was neither war
nor peace, tired with hanging traitors and the endless problem of her sister of Scotland, Elizabeth
saw no reason for refusing offers which would leave
her in peace for the rest of her own life. Philip, it
was said, would restore the Mass in the churches in
Holland. She might stipulate for such liberty of
conscience to the Holland Protestants as she was
herself willing to allow the English Catholics. She
saw no reason why she should insist on a liberty
of public worship which she had herself forbidden
at home. She did not see why the Hollanders
should be so precise about hearing Mass. She said
she would rather hear a thousand Masses herself
than have on her conscience the crimes committed
for the Mass or against it. She would not have her

realm in perpetual torment for Mr. Cecil's brothers in Christ.

This was Elizabeth's personal feeling. It could not be openly avowed. The States might then surrender to Philip in despair, and obtain better securities for their political liberties than she was ready to ask for them. They might then join the Spaniards and become her mortal enemies. But she had a high opinion of her own statecraft. Her Catholic friends assured her that, once at peace with Philip, she would be safe from all the world. At this moment accident revealed suddenly another chasm which was opening unsuspected at her feet.

Both Philip and she were really wishing for peace. A treaty of peace between the Catholic King and an excommunicated princess would end the dream of a Catholic revolution in England. If the English peers and gentry saw the censures of the Church set aside so lightly by the most ortho-dox prince in Europe, Parsons and his friends would preach in vain to them the obligation of rebellion. If this deadly negotiation was to be broken off, a blow must be struck, and struck at once. There was not a moment to be lost.

The enchanted prisoner at Tutbury was the sleeping and waking dream of Catholic chivalry. The brave knight who would slay the dragon, de-liver Mary Stuart, and place her on the usurper's throne, would outdo Orlando or St. George, and be sung of for ever as the noblest hero who had ever wielded brand or spear. Many a young British heart had thrilled with hope that for him the enterprise was reserved. One of these was a certain Anthony Babington, a gentleman of some fortune in Derbyshire. A seminary priest named Ballard, excited, like the rest, by the need of action, and anxious to prevent the peace, fell in with this Babington, and thought he had found the man for his work. Elizabeth dead and Mary Stuart free, there would be no more talk of peace. A plot was easily formed. Half a dozen gentlemen, five of them belonging to or connected with Elizabeth's own household, were to shoot or stab her and escape in the confusion; Babington was to make a dash on Mary Stuart's prison-house and carry her off to some safe place; while Ballard undertook to raise the Catholic peers and have her proclaimed queen. Elizabeth once removed, it was supposed that they would not hesitate. Parma would bring over the Spanish army from Dunkirk. The Protestants would be paralysed. All would be begun and ended in a few weeks or even days. The Catholic religion would be re-established and the hated heresy would be trampled out for ever. Mary Stuart had been consulted and had enthusiastically agreed.

This interesting lady had been lately profuse in her protestations of a desire for reconciliation with her dearest sister. Elizabeth had almost believed her sincere. Sick of the endless trouble with Mary

Stuart and her pretensions and schemings, she had intended that the Scotch queen should be included in the treaty with Philip, with an implied recognition of her right to succeed to the English throne after Elizabeth's death. It had been necessary, however, to ascertain in some way whether her protestations were sincere. A secret watch had been kept over her correspondence, and Babington's letters and her own answers had fallen into Walsingham's hands. There it all was in her own cipher, the key to which had been betrayed by the carelessness of a confederate. The six gentlemen who were to have rewarded Elizabeth's confidence by killing her were easily recognised. They were seized, with Babington and Ballard, when they imagined themselves on the eve of their triumph. Babington flinched and confessed, and they were all hanged. Mary Stuart herself had outworn compassion. Twice already on the discovery of her earlier plots the House of Commons had petitioned for her execution. For this last piece of treachery she was tried at Fotheringay before a commission of Peers and Privy Councillors. She denied her letters, but her complicity was proved beyond a doubt. Parliament was called, and a third time insisted that the long drama should now be ended and loyal England be allowed to breathe in peace. Elizabeth signed the warrant. France, Spain, any other power in the world would have long since made an end of a competitor so desperate and so incurable. Torn by many feelings—natural pity, dread of the world's opinion—Elizabeth paused before ordering the warrant to be executed. If nothing had been at stake but her own life, she would have left the lady to weave fresh plots and at last, perhaps, to succeed. If the nation's safety required an end to be made with her, she felt it hard that the duty should be thrown on herself. Where were all those eager champions who had signed the Association Bond, who had talked so loudly? Could none of them be found to recollect their oaths and take the law into their own hands?

Her Council, Burghley, and the rest, knowing her disposition and feeling that it was life or death to English liberty, took the responsibility on themselves. They sent the warrant down to Fotheringay at their own risk, leaving their mistress to deny, if she pleased, that she had meant it to be executed; and the wild career of Mary Stuart ended on the scaffold.

They knew what they were immediately doing. They knew that if treason had a meaning Mary Stuart had brought her fate upon herself. They did not, perhaps, realise the full effects that were to follow, or that with Mary Stuart had vanished the last serious danger of a Catholic insurrection in England; or perhaps they did realise it, and this was what decided them to act.

I cannot dwell on this here. As long as there was a Catholic princess of English blood to succeed

to the throne, the allegiance of the Catholics to
Elizabeth had been easily shaken. If she was
spared now, every one of them would look on her
as their future sovereign. To overthrow Elizabeth
might mean the loss of national independence.
The Queen of Scots gone, they were paralysed by
divided counsels, and love of country proved
stronger than their creed.

What concerns us specially at present is the
effect on the King of Spain. The reluctance of
Philip to undertake the English enterprise (the
'empresa,' as it was generally called) had arisen
from a fear that when it was accomplished he
would lose the fruit of his labours. He could
never assure himself that if he placed Mary Stuart
on the throne she would not become eventually
French. He now learnt that she had bequeathed
to himself her claims on the English succession.
He had once been titular King of England. He
had pretensions of his own, as in the descent from
Edward III. The Jesuits, the Catholic enthusiasts
throughout Europe, assured him that if he would
now take up the cause in earnest, he might make
England a province of Spain. There were still
difficulties. He might hope that the English
Catholic laity would accept him, but he could not
be sure of it. He could not be sure that he would
have the support of the Pope. He continued, as
the Conde de Feria said scornfully of him, 'meando
en vado,' a phrase which I cannot translate; it

meant hesitating when he ought to act. But he saw, or thought he saw, that he could now take a stronger attitude towards Elizabeth as a claimant to her throne. If the treaty of peace was to go forward, he could raise his terms. He could insist on the restoration of the Catholic religion in England. The States of the Low Countries had made over five of their strongest towns to Elizabeth as the price of her assistance. He could insist on her restoring them, not to the States, but to himself. Could she be brought to consent to such an act of perfidy, Parma and he both felt that the power would then be gone from her, as effectually as Samson's when his locks were clipped by the harlot, and they could leave her then, if it suited them, on a throne which would have become a pillory—for the finger of scorn to point at.

With such a view before him it was more than ever necessary for Philip to hurry forward the preparations which he had already commenced. The more formidable he could make himself, the better able he would be to frighten Elizabeth into submission.

Every dockyard in Spain was set to work, building galleons and collecting stores. Santa Cruz would command. Philip was himself more resolved than ever to accompany the expedition in person and dictate from the English Channel the conditions of the pacification of Europe.

Secrecy was no longer attempted—indeed, was

no longer possible. All Latin Christendom was palpitating with expectation. At Lisbon, at Cadiz, at Barcelona, at Naples, the shipwrights were busy night and day. The sea was covered with vessels freighted with arms and provisions streaming to the mouth of the Tagus. Catholic volunteers from all nations flocked into the Peninsula, to take a share in the mighty movement which was to decide the fate of the world, and bishops, priests, and monks were set praying through the whole Latin Communion that Heaven would protect its own cause.

Meantime the negotiations for peace continued, and Elizabeth, strange to say, persisted in listening. She would not see what was plain to all the world besides. The execution of the Queen of Scots lay on her spirit and threw her back into the obstinate humour which had made Walsingham so often despair of her safety. For two months after that scene at Fotheringay she had refused to see Burghley, and would consult no one but Sir James Crofts and her Spanish-tempered ladies. She knew that Spain now intended that she should betray the towns in the Low Countries, yet she was blind to the infamy which it would bring upon her. She left her troops there without their wages to shiver into mutiny. She named commissioners, with Sir James Crofts at their head, to go to Ostend and treat with Parma, and if she had not resolved on an act of treachery she at least played with the temptation, and persuaded herself that if she chose to make over the towns to Philip, she would be only restoring them to their lawful owner.

Burghley and Walsingham, you can see from their letters, believed now that Elizabeth had ruined herself at last. Happily her moods were variable as the weather. She was forced to see the condition to which she had reduced her affairs in the Low Countries by the appearance of a number of starving wretches who had deserted from the garrisons there and had come across to clamour for their pay at her own palace gates. If she had no troops in the field but a mutinous and starving rabble, she might get no terms at all. It might be well to show Philip that on one element at least she could still be dangerous. She had lost nothing by the bold actions of Drake and the privateers. With half a heart she allowed Drake to fit them out again, take the *Buonaventura*, a ship of her own, to carry his flag, and go down to the coast of Spain and see what was going on. He was not to do too much. She sent a vice-admiral with him, in the *Lion*, to be a check on over-audacity. Drake knew how to deal with embarrassing vice-admirals. His own adventurers would sail, if he ordered, to the Mountains of the Moon, and be quite certain that it was the right place to go to. Once under way and on the blue water he would go his own course and run his own risks. Cadiz Harbour was thronged with transports, provision

ships, powder vessels—a hundred sail of them—
many of a thousand tons and over, loading with
stores for the Armada. There were thirty sail of
adventurers, the smartest ships afloat on the ocean,
and sailed by the smartest seamen that ever handled rope or tiller. Something might be done at
Cadiz if he did not say too much about it. The
leave had been given to him to go, but he knew by
experience, and Burghley again warned him, that
it might, and probably would, be revoked if he
waited too long. The moment was his own, and he
used it. He was but just in time. Before his sails
were under the horizon a courier galloped into Plymouth with orders that under no condition was he
to enter port or haven of the King of Spain, or in-
jure Spanish subjects. What else was he going
out for? He had guessed how it would be. Comedy
or earnest he could not tell. If earnest, some such
order would be sent after him, and he had not an
instant to lose.

He sailed on the morning of the 12th of April.
Off Ushant he fell in with a north-west gale, and
he flew on, spreading every stitch of canvas which
his spars would bear. In five days he was at Cape
St. Vincent. On the 18th he had the white houses
of Cadiz right in front of him, and could see for
himself the forests of masts from the ships and
transports with which the harbour was choked.
Here was a chance for a piece of service if there
was courage for the venture. He signalled for his

officers to come on board the *Buonaventura*.
There before their eyes was, if not the Armada itself,
the materials which were to fit the Armada for the
seas.   Did they dare to go in with him and destroy
them ?   There were batteries at the harbour mouth,
but Drake's mariners had faced Spanish batteries
at St. Domingo and Carthagena and had not
found them very formidable.   Go in ?   Of course
they would.   Where Drake would lead the corsairs
of Plymouth were never afraid to follow.   The
vice-admiral pleaded danger to her Majesty's ships.
It was not the business of an English fleet to be
particular about danger.   Straight in they went
with a fair wind and a flood tide, ran past the
batteries and under a storm of shot, to which they
did not trouble themselves to wait to reply.   The
poor vice-admiral followed reluctantly in the *Lion*.
A single shot hit the *Lion*, and he edged away
out of range, anchored, and drifted to sea again
with the ebb   But Drake and all the rest dashed
on, sank the guardship—a large galleon—and sent
flying a fleet of galleys which ventured too near
them and were never seen again.

Further resistance there was none—absolutely
none.   The crews of the store ships escaped in
their boats to land.   The governor of Cadiz, the
same Duke of Medina Sidonia who the next year
was to gain a disastrous immortality, fled 'like a tall
gentleman' to raise troops and prevent Drake from
landing.   Drake had no intention of landing.   At

N

his extreme leisure he took possession of the
Spanish shipping, searched every vessel, and carried
off everything that he could use. He detained as
prisoners the few men that he found on board, and
then, after doing his work deliberately and completely, he set the hulls on fire, cut the cables, and
left them to drive on the rising tide under the
walls of the town—a confused mass of blazing ruin.
On the 12th of April he had sailed from Plymouth ;
on the 19th he entered Cadiz harbour ; on the 1st of
May he passed out again without the loss of a boat
or a man. He said in jest that he had singed the
King of Spain's beard for him. In sober prose he
had done the King of Spain an amount of damage
which a million ducats and a year's labour would
imperfectly replace. The daring rapidity of the
enterprise astonished Spain, and astonished Europe
more than the storm of the West Indian towns.
The English had long teeth, as Santa Cruz had
told Philip's council, and the teeth would need
drawing before Mass would be heard again at
Westminster. The Spaniards were a gallant race,
and a dashing exploit, though at their own expense,
could be admired by the countrymen of Cervantes.
' So praised,' we read, ' was Drake for his valour
among them that they said if he was not a Lutheran
there would not be the like of him in the world.'
A Court lady was invited by the King to join a
party on a lake near Madrid. The lady replied
that she dared not trust herself on the water with

his Majesty lest Sir Francis Drake should have
her.

Drake might well be praised. But Drake
would have been the first to divide the honour with
the comrades who were his arm and hand. Great
admirals and generals do not win their battles
single-handed like the heroes of romance   Orders
avail only when there are men to execute them.
Not a captain, not an officer who served under
Drake, ever flinched or blundered. Never was
such a school for seamen as that twenty years'
privateering war between the servants of the Pope
and the West-country Protestant adventurers.
Those too must be remembered who built and
rigged the ships in which they sailed and fought
their battles. We may depend upon it that there
was no dishonesty in contractors, no scamping of
the work in the yards where the Plymouth rovers
were fitted out for sea. Their hearts were in it;
they were soldiers of a common cause.

Three weeks had sufficed for Cadiz. No order
for recall had yet arrived. Drake had other plans
before him, and the men were in high spirits and
ready for anything. A fleet of Spanish men-of-war
was expected round from the Mediterranean. He
proposed to stay for a week or two in the neighbourhood of the Straits, in the hope of falling in
with them. He wanted fresh water, too, and had
to find it somewhere.

Before leaving Cadiz Roads he had to decide

what to do with his prisoners. Many English were known to be in the hands of the Holy Office working in irons as galley slaves. He sent in a pinnace to propose an exchange, and had to wait some days for an answer. At length, after a reference to Lisbon, the Spanish authorities replied that they had no English prisoners. If this was true those they had must have died of barbarous usage; and after a consultation with his officers Sir Francis sent in word that for the future such prisoners as they might take would be sold to the Moors, and the money applied to the redemption of English captives in other parts of the world.

Water was the next point. There were springs at Faro, with a Spanish force stationed there to guard them. Force or no force, water was to be had. The boats were sent on shore. The boats' crews stormed the forts and filled the casks. The vice-admiral again lifted up his voice. The Queen had ordered that there was to be no landing on Spanish soil. At Cadiz the order had been observed. There had been no need to land. Here at Faro there had been direct defiance of her Majesty's command. He became so loud in his clamours that Drake found it necessary to lock him up in his own cabin, and at length to send him home with his ship to complain. For himself, as the expected fleet from the Straits did not appear, and as he had shaken off his troublesome second in command, he proceeded leisurely up the coast,

intending to look in at Lisbon and see for himself
how things were going on there. All along as he
went he fell in with traders loaded with supplies
for the use of the Armada. All these he destroyed
as he advanced, and at length found himself under
the purple hills of Cintra and looking up into the
Tagus. There lay gathered together the strength
of the fighting naval force of Spain—fifty great
galleons, already arrived, the largest warships
which then floated on the ocean. Santa Cruz,
the best officer in the Spanish navy, was himself
in the town and in command. To venture a
repetition of the Cadiz exploit in the face of such
odds seemed too desperate even for Drake, but it
was one of those occasions when the genius of a
great commander sees more than ordinary eyes.
He calculated, and, as was proved afterwards,
calculated rightly, that the galleons would be half
manned, or not manned at all, and crowded with
landsmen bringing on board the stores. Their
sides as they lay would be choked with hulks and
lighters. They would be unable to get their
anchors up, set their canvas, or stir from their
moorings. Daring as Drake was known to be, no
one would expect him to go with so small a force
into the enemy's stronghold, and there would be
no preparations to meet him. He could count
upon the tides. The winds at that season of the
year were fresh and steady, and could be counted
on also to take him in or out ; there was sea room

in the river for such vessels as the adventurers' to manœuvre and to retreat if overmatched. Rash as such an enterprise might seem to an unprofessional eye, Drake certainly thought of it, perhaps had meant to try it in some form or other and so make an end of the Spanish invasion of England. He could not venture without asking first for his mistress's permission. He knew her nature. He knew that his services at Cadiz would outweigh his disregard of her orders, and that so far he had nothing to fear; but he knew also that she was still hankering after peace, and that without her leave he must do nothing to make peace impossible. There is a letter from him to the Queen, written when he was lying off Lisbon, very characteristic of the time and the man.

Nelson or Lord St. Vincent did not talk much of expecting supernatural assistance. If they had we should suspect them of using language conventionally which they would have done better to leave alone. Sir Francis Drake, like his other great contemporaries, believed that he was engaged in a holy cause, and was not afraid or ashamed to say so. His object was to protest against a recall in the flow of victory. The Spaniards, he said, were but mortal men. They were enemies of the Truth, upholders of Dagon's image, which had fallen in other days before the Ark, and would fall again if boldly defied. So long as he had ships that would float, and there was food on board them for the men to eat, he entreated her to let him stay and strike whenever a chance was offered him. The continuing to the end yielded the true glory. When men were serving religion and their country, a merciful God, it was likely, would give them victory, and Satan and his angels should not prevail. All in good time. Another year and Drake would have the chance he wanted. For the moment Satan had prevailed—Satan in the shape of Elizabeth's Catholic advisers. Her answer came. It was warm and generous. She did not, could not, blame him for what he had done so far, but she desired him to provoke the King of Spain no further. The negotiations for peace had opened, and must not be interfered with.

This prohibition from the Queen prevented, perhaps, what would have been the most remarkable exploit in English naval history. As matters stood it would have been perfectly possible for Drake to have gone into the Tagus, and if he could not have burnt the galleons he could certainly have come away unhurt. He had guessed their condition with entire correctness. The ships were there, but the ships' companies were not on board them. Santa Cruz himself admitted that if Drake had gone in he could have himself done nothing ' por falta de gente ' (for want of men). And Drake undoubtedly would have gone, and would have done something with which all the world would have rung, but for the positive command of his mistress. He lingered in the roads at Cintra, hoping that Santa Cruz would come out and meet him. All Spain was clamouring at Santa Cruz's inaction. Philip wrote to stir the old admiral to energy. He must not allow himself to be defied by a squadron of insolent rovers. He must chase them off the coast or destroy them. Santa Cruz needed no stirring. Santa Cruz, the hero of a hundred fights, was chafing at his own impotence; but he was obliged to tell his master that if he wished to have service out of his galleons he must provide crews to handle them, and they must rot at their anchors till he did. He told him, moreover, that it was time for him to exert himself in earnest. If he waited much longer, England would have grown too strong for him to deal with.

In strict obedience Drake ought now to have gone home, but the campaign had brought so far more glory than prize money. His comrades required some consolation for their disappointment at Lisbon. The theory of these armaments of the adventurers was that the cost should be paid somehow by the enemy, and he could be assured that if he brought back a prize or two in which she could claim a share the Queen would not call him to a very strict account. Homeward-bound galleons or merchantmen were to be met with occasionally at the Azores. On leaving Lisbon Drake headed away to St. Michael's, and his lucky star was still in the ascendant.

As if sent on purpose for him, the *San Philip*, a magnificent caraque from the Indies, fell straight into his hands, 'so richly loaded,' it was said, 'that every man in the fleet counted his fortune made.' There was no need to wait for more. It was but two months since Drake had sailed from Plymouth. He could now go home after a cruise of which the history of his own or any other country had never presented the like. He had struck the King of Spain in his own stronghold. He had disabled the intended Armada for one season at least. He had picked up a prize by the way and as if by accident, worth half a million, to pay his expenses, so that he had cost nothing to his mistress, and had brought back a handsome present for her. I doubt if such a naval estimate was ever presented to an English House of Commons. Above all he had taught the self-confident Spaniard to be afraid of him, and he carried back his poor comrades in such a glow of triumph that they would have fought Satan and all his angels with Drake at their head.

Our West-country annals still tell how the country people streamed down in their best clothes to see the great *San Philip* towed into Dartmouth Harbour. English Protestantism was no bad cable for the nation to ride by in those stormy times, and deserves to be honourably remembered in a School of History at an English University.

LECTURE VIII

SAILING OF THE ARMADA

PEACE or war between Spain and England, that
was now the question, with a prospect of securing
the English succession for himself or one of his
daughters. With the whole Spanish nation smarting under the indignity of the burning of the ships
at Cadiz, Philip's warlike ardour had warmed into
something like fire. He had resolved at any rate,
if he was to forgive his sister-in-law at all, to insist
on more than toleration for the Catholics in England. He did not contemplate as even possible
that the English privateers, however bold or dexterous, could resist such an armament as he was
preparing to lead to the Channel. The Royal
Navy, he knew very well, did not exceed twenty-
five ships of all sorts and sizes. The adventurers
might be equal to sudden daring actions, but would
and must be crushed by such a fleet as was being
fitted out at Lisbon. He therefore, for himself,
meant to demand that the Catholic religion should
be restored to its complete and exclusive superiority,
and certain towns in England were to be made
over to be garrisoned by Spanish troops as securities

for Elizabeth's good behaviour. As often happens with irresolute men, when they have once been forced to a decision they are as too hasty as before they were too slow. After Drake had retired from Lisbon the King of Spain sent orders to the Prince of Parma not to wait for the arrival of the Armada, but to cross the Channel immediately with the Flanders army, and bring Elizabeth to her knees. Parma had more sense than his master. He represented that he could not cross without a fleet to cover his passage. His transport barges would only float in smooth water, and whether the water was smooth or rough they could be sent to the bottom by half a dozen English cruisers from the Thames. Supposing him to have landed, either in Thanet or other spot, he reminded Philip that he could not have at most more than 25,000 men with him. The English militia were in training. The Jesuits said they were disaffected, but the Jesuits might be making a mistake. He might have to fight more than one battle. He would have to leave detachments as he advanced to London, to cover his communications, and a reverse would be fatal. He would obey if his Majesty persisted, but he recommended Philip to continue to amuse the English with the treaty till the Armada was ready, and, in evident consciousness that the enterprise would be harder than Philip imagined, he even gave it as his own opinion still (notwithstanding Cadiz), that if Elizabeth would surrender the cautionary towns in Flanders to Spain, and would grant the English Catholics a fair degree of liberty, it would be Philip's interest to make peace at once without stipulating for further terms. He could make a new war if he wished at a future time, when circumstances might be more convenient and the Netherlands revolt subdued.

To such conditions as these it seemed that Elizabeth was inclining to consent. The towns had been trusted to her keeping by the Netherlanders. To give them up to the enemy to make better conditions for herself would be an infamy so great as to have disgraced Elizabeth for ever; yet she would not see it. She said the towns belonged to Philip and she would only be restoring his own to him. Burghley bade her, if she wanted peace, send back Drake to the Azores and frighten Philip for his gold ships. She was in one of her ungovernable moods. Instead of sending out Drake again she ordered her own fleet to be dismantled and laid up at Chatham, and she condescended to apologise to Parma for the burning of the transports at Cadiz as done against her orders.

This was in December 1587, only five months before the Armada sailed from Lisbon. Never had she brought herself and her country so near ruin. The entire safety of England rested at that moment on the adventurers, and on the adventurers alone.

Meanwhile, with enormous effort the destruction

at Cadiz had been repaired. The great fleet was
pushed on, and in February Santa Cruz reported
himself almost ready. Santa Cruz and Philip,
however, were not in agreement as to what should
be done. Santa Cruz was a fighting admiral,
Philip was not a fighting king. He changed his
mind as often as Elizabeth. Hot fits varied with
cold. His last news from England led him to hope
that fighting would not be wanted. The Commissioners were sitting at Ostend. On one side there
were the formal negotiations, in which the surrender
of the towns was not yet treated as an open question. Had the States been aware that Elizabeth
was even in thought entertaining it, they would
have made terms instantly on their own account
and left her alone in the cold. Besides this, there
was a second negotiation underneath, carried on by
private agents, in which the surrender was to be
the special condition. These complicated schemings Parma purposely protracted, to keep Elizabeth
in false security. She had not deliberately intended
to give up the towns. At the last moment she
would have probably refused, unless the States
themselves consented to it as part of a general
settlement. But she was playing with the idea.
The States, she thought, were too obstinate. Peace
would be good for them, and she said she might do
them good if she pleased, whether they liked it or
not.

Parma was content that she should amuse her-

self with words and neglect her defences by sea and
land. By the end of February Santa Cruz was
ready. A northerly wind blows strong down the
coast of Portugal in the spring months, and he
meant to be off before it set in, before the end of
March at latest. Unfortunately for Spain, Santa
Cruz fell ill at the last moment—ill, it was said,
with anxiety. Santa Cruz knew well enough what
Philip would not know—that the expedition would
be no holiday parade. He had reason enough to
be anxious if Philip was to accompany him and tie
his hands and embarrass him. Any way, Santa
Cruz died after a few days' illness. The sailing
had to be suspended till a new commander could
be decided on, and in the choice which Philip
made he gave a curious proof of what he intended
the expedition to do. He did not really expect or
wish for any serious fighting. He wanted to be
sovereign of England again, with the assent of the
English Catholics. He did not mean, if he could
help it, to irritate the national pride by force and
conquest. While Santa Cruz lived, Spanish public
opinion would not allow him to be passed over.
Santa Cruz must command, and Philip had resolved
to go with him, to prevent too violent proceedings.
Santa Cruz dead, he could find someone who would
do what he was told, and his own presence would
no longer be necessary.

The Duke of Medina Sidonia, named El Bueno,
or the Good, was a grandee of highest rank. He

was enormously rich, fond of hunting and shooting, a tolerable rider, for the rest a harmless creature getting on to forty, conscious of his defects, but not aware that so great a prince had any need to mend them; without vanity, without ambition, and most happy when lounging in his orange gardens at San Lucan. Of active service he had seen none. He was Captain-General of Andalusia, and had run away from Cadiz when Drake came into the harbour; but that was all. To his astonishment and to his dismay he learnt that it was on him that the choice had fallen to be the Lord High Admiral of Spain and commander of the so much talked of expedition to England. He protested his unfitness. He said that he was no seaman; that he knew nothing of fighting by sea or land; that if he ventured out in a boat he was always sick; that he had never seen the English Channel; and that, as to politics, he neither knew anything nor cared anything about them. In short, he had not one qualification which such a post required.

Philip liked his modesty; but in fact the Duke's defects were his recommendations. He would obey his instructions, would not fight unless it was necessary, and would go into no rash adventures. All that Philip wanted him to do was to find the Prince of Parma, and act as Parma should bid him. As to seamanship, he would have the best officers in the navy under him; and for a second in command he should have Don Diego de Valdez, a cautious, silent, sullen old sailor, a man after Philip's own heart.

Doubting, hesitating, the Duke repaired to Lisbon. There he was put in better heart by a nun, who said Our Lady had sent her to promise him success. Every part of the service was new to him. He was a fussy, anxious little man; set himself to inquire into everything, to meddle with things which he could not understand and had better have left alone. He ought to have left details to the responsible heads of departments. He fancied that in a week or two he could look himself into everything. There were 130 ships, 8,000 seamen, 19,000 Spanish infantry, with gentlemen volunteers, officers, priests, surgeons, galley slaves—at least 3,000 more—provisioned for six months. Then there were the ships' stores, arms small and great, powder, spars, cordage, canvas, and such other million necessities as ships on service need. The whole of this the poor Duke took on himself to examine into, and, as he could not understand what he saw, and knew not what to look at, nothing was examined into at all. Everyone's mind was, in fact, so much absorbed by the spiritual side of the thing that they could not attend to vulgar commonplaces. Don Quixote, when he set out on his expedition, and forgot money and a change of linen, was not in a state of wilder exaltation than Catholic Europe at the sailing of the Armada. Every noble family in

Spain had sent one or other of its sons to fight for
Christ and Our Lady.

For three years the stream of prayer had been
ascending from church, cathedral, or oratory. The
King had emptied his treasury. The hidalgo and
the tradesman had offered their contributions. The
crusade against the Crescent itself had not kindled
a more intense or more sacred enthusiasm. All
pains were taken to make the expedition spiritually
worthy of its purpose. No impure thing, specially
no impure woman, was to approach the yards or
ships. Swearing, quarrelling, gambling, were prohi-
bited under terrible penalties. The galleons were
named after the apostles and saints to whose charge
they were committed, and every seaman and soldier
confessed and communicated on going on board.
The shipboys at sunrise were to sing their Buenos
Dias at the foot of the mainmast, and their Ave
Maria as the sun sank into the ocean. On the
Imperial banner were embroidered the figures of
Christ and His Mother, and as a motto the haughty
'Plus Ultra' of Charles V. was replaced with the
more pious aspiration, 'Exsurge, Deus, et vindica
causam tuam.'

Nothing could be better if the more vulgar
necessities had been looked to equally well. Unluckily, Medina Sidonia had taken the inspection of
these on himself, and Medina Sidonia was unable
to correct the information which any rascal chose
to give him.

o

At length, at the end of April, he reported himself satisfied. The banner was blessed in the cathedral, men and stores all on board, and the Invincible Armada prepared to go upon its way. No wonder Philip was confident. A hundred and thirty galleons, from 1,300 to 700 tons, 30,000 fighting men, besides slaves and servants, made up a force which the world might well think invincible. The guns were the weakest part. There were twice as many as the English; but they were for the most part nine and six pounders, and with but fifty rounds to each. The Spaniards had done their sea fighting hitherto at close range, grappling and trusting to musketry. They were to receive a lesson about this before the summer was over. But Philip himself meanwhile expected evidently that he would meet with no opposition. Of priests he had provided 180; of surgeons and surgeons' assistants eighty-five only for the whole fleet.

In the middle of May he sent down his last orders. The Duke was not to seek a battle. If he fell in with Drake he was to take no notice of him, but thank God, as Dogberry said to the watchman, that he was rid of a knave. He was to go straight to the North Foreland, there anchor and communicate with Parma. The experienced admirals who had learnt their trade under Santa Cruz—Martinez de Recalde, Pedro de Valdez, Miguel de Oquendo —strongly urged the securing Plymouth or the Isle of Wight on their way up Channel. This had

evidently been Santa Cruz's own design, and the
only rational one to have followed. Philip did not
see it. He did not believe it would prove necessary; but as to this and as to fighting he left them,
as he knew he must do, a certain discretion.

The Duke then, flying the sacred banner on
the *San Martin*, dropped down the Tagus on the
14th of May, followed by the whole fleet. The
San Martin had been double-timbered with oak,
to keep the shot out. He liked his business no
better. In vain he repeated to himself that it was
God's cause. God would see they came to no harm.
He was no sooner in the open sea than he found
no cause, however holy, saved men from the consequences of their own blunders. They were late out,
and met the north trade wind, as Santa Cruz had
foretold.

They drifted to leeward day by day till they had
dropped down to Cape St. Vincent. Infinite pains
had been taken with the spiritual state of every one
on board. The carelessness or roguery of contractors and purveyors had not been thought of. The
water had been taken in three months before. It
was found foul and stinking. The salt beef, the
salt pork, and fish were putrid, the bread full of
maggots and cockroaches. Cask was opened after
cask. It was the same story everywhere. They
had to be all thrown overboard. In the whole fleet
there was not a sound morsel of food but biscuit
and dried fruit. The men went down in hundreds

with dysentery. The Duke bewailed his fate as
innocently as Sancho Panza. He hoped God would
help. He had wished no harm to anybody. He
had left his home and his family to please the King,
and he trusted the King would remember it. He
wrote piteously for fresh stores, if the King would
not have them all perish. The admirals said they
could go no further without fresh water. All was
dismay and confusion. The wind at last fell round
south, and they made Finisterre. It then came on
to blow, and they were scattered. The Duke with
half the fleet crawled into Corunna, the crews
scarce able to man the yards and trying to desert
in shoals.

The missing ships dropped in one by one, but a
week passed and a third of them were still absent.
Another despairing letter went off from the Duke
to his master. He said that he concluded from
their misfortunes that God disapproved of the
expedition, and that it had better be abandoned.
Diego Florez was of the same opinion. The stores
were worthless, he said. The men were sick and
out of heart. Nothing could be done that season.

It was not by flinching at the first sight of
difficulty that the Spaniards had become masters
of half the world. The old comrades of Santa
Cruz saw nothing in what had befallen them beyond a common accident of sea life. To abandon
at the first check an enterprise undertaken with so
much pretence, they said, would be cowardly and

dishonourable. Ships were not lost because they were out of sight. Fresh meat and bread could be taken on board from Corunna. They could set up a shore hospital for the sick. The sickness was not dangerous. There had been no deaths. A little energy and all would be well again. Pedro de Valdez despatched a courier to Philip to entreat him not to listen to the Duke's croakings. Philip returned a speedy answer telling the Duke not to be frightened at shadows.

There was nothing, in fact, really to be alarmed at. Fresh water took away the dysentery. Fresh food was brought in from the country. Galician seamen filled the gaps made by the deserters. The ships were laid on shore and scraped and tallowed. Tents were pitched on an island in the harbour, with altars and priests, and everyone confessed again and received the Sacrament. 'This,' wrote the Duke, ' is great riches and a precious jewel, and all now are well content and cheerful.' The scattered flock had reassembled. Damages were all repaired, and the only harm had been loss of time. Once more, on the 23rd of July, the Armada in full numbers was under way for England and streaming across the Bay of Biscay with a fair wind for the mouth of the Channel.

Leaving the Duke for the moment, we must now glance at the preparations made in England to receive him. It might almost be said that there were none at all. The winter months had

been wild and changeable, but not so wild and not
so fluctuating as the mind of England's mistress.
In December her fleet had been paid off at Chatham. The danger of leaving the country without
any regular defence was pressed on her so vehemently that she consented to allow part of the
ships to be recommissioned. The *Revenge* was
given to Drake. He and Howard, the Lord
Admiral, were to have gone with a mixed squadron
from the Royal Navy and the adventurers down to
the Spanish coast. In every loyal subject there
had long been but one opinion, that a good open
war was the only road to an honourable peace.
The open war, they now trusted, was come at last.
But the hope was raised only to be disappointed.
With the news of Santa Cruz's death came a report
which Elizabeth greedily believed, that the Armada
was dissolving and was not coming at all. Sir
James Crofts sang the usual song that Drake and
Howard wanted war, because war was their trade.
She recalled her orders. She said that she was
assured of peace in six weeks, and that beyond that
time the services of the fleet would not be required.
Half the men engaged were to be dismissed at
once to save their pay. Drake and Lord Henry
Seymour might cruise with four or five of the
Queen's ships between Plymouth and the Solent.
Lord Howard was to remain in the Thames with
the rest. I know not whether swearing was
interdicted in the English navy as well as in the

Spanish, but I will answer for it that Howard did not spare his language when this missive reached him. ' Never,' he said, ' since England was England was such a stratagem made to deceive us as this treaty. We have not hands left to carry the ships back to Chatham. We are like bears tied to a stake; the Spaniards may come to worry us like dogs, and we cannot hurt them.'

It was well for England that she had other defenders than the wildly managed navy of the Queen. Historians tell us how the gentlemen of the coast came out in their own vessels to meet the invaders. Come they did, but who were they? Ships that could fight the Spanish galleons were not made in a day or a week. They were built already. They were manned by loyal subjects, the business of whose lives had been to meet the enemies of their land and faith on the wide ocean— not by those who had been watching with divided hearts for a Catholic revolution.

March went by, and sure intelligence came that the Armada was not dissolving. Again Drake prayed the Queen to let him take the *Revenge* and the Western adventurers down to Lisbon; but the commissioners wrote full of hope from Ostend, and Elizabeth was afraid ' the King of Spain might take it ill.' She found fault with Drake's expenses. She charged him with wasting her ammunition in target practice. She had it doled out to him in driblets, and allowed no more than would serve for a day and a half's service. She kept a sharp hand on the victualling houses. April went, and her four finest ships—the *Triumph*, the *Victory*, the *Elizabeth Jonas*, and the *Bear*—were still with sails unbent, 'keeping Chatham church.' She said they would not be wanted and it would be waste of money to refit them. Again she was forced to yield at last, and the four ships were got to sea in time, the workmen in the yards making up for the delay; but she had few enough when her whole fleet was out upon the Channel, and but for the privateers there would have been an ill reckoning when the trial came. The Armada was coming now. There was no longer a doubt of it. Lord Henry Seymour was left with five Queen's ships and thirty London adventurers to watch Parma and the Narrow Seas. Howard, carrying his own flag in the *Ark Raleigh*, joined Drake at Plymouth with seventeen others.

Still the numbing hand of his mistress pursued him. Food supplies had been issued to the middle of June, and no more was to be allowed. The weather was desperate—wildest summer ever known. The south-west gales brought the Atlantic rollers into the Sound. Drake lay inside, perhaps behind the island which bears his name. Howard rode out the gales under Mount Edgecumbe, the days going by and the provisions wasting. The rations were cut down to make the stores last longer. Owing to the many changes the crews had been hastily raised. They were ill-clothed, ill-provided every way, but they complained of nothing, caught fish to mend their mess dinners, and prayed only for the speedy coming of the enemy. Even Howard's heart failed him now. English sailors would do what could be done by man, but they could not fight with famine. 'Awake, Madam,' he wrote to the Queen, 'awake, for the love of Christ, and see the villainous treasons round about you.' He goaded her into ordering supplies for one more month, but this was to be positively the last. The victuallers inquired if they should make further preparations. She answered peremptorily, 'No'; and again the weeks ran on. The contractors, it seemed, had caught her spirit, for the beer which had been furnished for the fleet turned sour, and those who drank it sickened. The officers, on their own responsibility, ordered wine and arrowroot for the sick out of Plymouth, to be called to a sharp account when all was over. Again the rations were reduced. Four weeks' allowance was stretched to serve for six, and still the Spaniards did not come. So England's forlorn hope was treated at the crisis of her destiny. The preparations on land were scarcely better. The militia had been called out. A hundred thousand men had given their names, and the stations had been arranged where they were to assemble if the enemy attempted a landing. But there were no reserves, no magazines of arms, no stores or tents, no requisites for an army save the men themselves and what local resources could furnish. For a general the Queen had chosen the Earl of Leicester, who might have the merit of fidelity to herself, but otherwise was the worst fitted that she could have found in her whole dominions; and the Prince of Parma was coming, if he came at all, at the head of the best-provided and best-disciplined troops in Europe. The hope of England at that moment was in her patient suffering sailors at Plymouth. Each morning they looked out passionately for the Spanish sails. Time was a worse enemy than the galleons. The six weeks would be soon gone, and the Queen's ships must then leave the seas if the crews were not to starve. Drake had certain news that the Armada had sailed. Where was it? Once he dashed out as far as Ushant, but turned back, lest it should pass him in the night and find Plymouth undefended; and smaller grew the messes and leaner and paler the seamen's faces. Still not a man murmured or gave in. They had no leisure to be sick.

The last week of July had now come. There were half-rations for one week more, and powder for two days' fighting. That was all. On so light a thread such mighty issues were now depending. On Friday, the 23rd, the Armada had started for the second time, the numbers undiminished; religious fervour burning again, and heart and hope high as ever. Saturday, Sunday, and Monday they

sailed on with a smooth sea and soft south winds,
and on Monday night the Duke found himself at
the Channel mouth with all his flock about him.
Tuesday morning the wind shifted to the north,
then backed to the west, and blew hard. The sea
got up, broke into the stern galleries of the galleons,
and sent the galleys looking for shelter in French
harbours. The fleet hove to for a couple of days,
till the weather mended. On Friday afternoon
they sighted the Lizard and formed into fighting
order ; the Duke in the centre, Alonzo de Leyva
leading in a vessel of his own called the *Rata
Coronada*, Don Martin de Recalde covering the
rear. The entire line stretched to about seven
miles.

The sacred banner was run up to the masthead
of the *San Martin*. Each ship saluted with all
her guns, and every man—officer, noble, seaman,
or slave—knelt on the decks at a given signal to
commend themselves to Mary and her Son. We
shall miss the meaning of this high epic story if we
do not realise that both sides had the most profound
conviction that they were fighting the battle of the
Almighty. Two principles, freedom and authority,
were contending for the guidance of mankind.
In the evening the Duke sent off two fast fly-boats
to Parma to announce his arrival in the Channel,
with another reporting progress to Philip, and saying that till he heard from the Prince he meant to
stop at the Isle of Wight. It is commonly said

that his officers advised him to go in and take Plymouth. There is no evidence for this. The island would have been a far more useful position for them.

At dark that Friday night the beacons were seen blazing all up the coast and inland on the tops of the hills. They crept on slowly through Saturday, with reduced canvas, feeling their way—not a sail to be seen. At midnight a pinnace brought in a fishing boat, from which they learnt that on the sight of the signal fires the English had come out that morning from Plymouth. Presently, when the moon rose, they saw sails passing between them and the land. With daybreak the whole scene became visible, and the curtain lifted on the first act of the drama. The Armada was between Rame Head and the Eddystone, or a little to the west of it. Plymouth Sound was right open to their left. The breeze, which had dropped in the night, was freshening from the south-west, and right ahead of them, outside the Mew Stone, were eleven ships manœuvring to recover the wind. Towards the land were some forty others, of various sizes, and this formed, as far as they could see, the whole English force. In numbers the Spaniards were nearly three to one. In the size of the ships there was no comparison. With these advantages the Duke decided to engage, and a signal was made to hold the wind and keep the enemy apart. The eleven ships ahead were Howard's squadron; those inside were Drake and the adventurers. With some surprise the Spanish officers saw Howard reach easily to windward out of range and join Drake. The whole English fleet then passed out close-hauled in line behind them and swept along their rear, using guns more powerful than theirs and pouring in broadsides from safe distance with deadly effect. Recalde, with Alonzo de Leyva and Oquendo, who came to his help, tried desperately to close; but they could make nothing of it. They were out-sailed and out-cannoned. The English fired five shots to one of theirs, and the effect was the more destructive because, as with Rodney's action at Dominica, the galleons were crowded with troops, and shot and splinters told terribly among them.

The experience was new and not agreeable. Recalde's division was badly cut up, and a Spaniard present observes that certain officers showed cowardice—a hit at the Duke, who had kept out of fire. The action lasted till four in the afternoon. The wind was then freshening fast and the sea rising. Both fleets had by this time passed the Sound, and the Duke, seeing that nothing could be done, signalled to bear away up Channel, the English following two miles astern. Recalde's own ship had been an especial sufferer. She was observed to be leaking badly, to drop behind, and to be in danger of capture. Pedro de Valdez wore round to help him in the *Capitana*, of the Andalusian squadron, fouled the *Santa Catalina* in turning, broke his bowsprit and foretopmast, and became unmanageable. The Andalusian *Capitana* was one of the finest ships in the Spanish fleet, and Don Pedro one of the ablest and most popular commanders. She had 500 men on board, a large sum of money, and, among other treasures, a box of jewel-hilted swords, which Philip was sending over to the English Catholic peers. But it was growing dark. Sea and sky looked ugly. The Duke was flurried, and signalled to go on and leave Don Pedro to his fate. Alonzo de Leyva and Oquendo rushed on board the *San Martin* to protest. It was no use. Diego Florez said he could not risk the safety of the fleet for a single officer. The deserted *Capitana* made a brave defence, but could not save herself, and fell, with the jewelled swords, 50,000 ducats, and a welcome supply of powder, into Drake's hands.

Off the Start there was a fresh disaster. Every one was in ill-humour. A quarrel broke out between the soldiers and seamen in Oquendo's galleon. He was himself still absent. Some wretch or other flung a torch into the powder magazine and jumped overboard. The deck was blown off, and 200 men along with it.

Two such accidents following an unsuccessful engagement did not tend to reconcile the Spaniards to the Duke's command. Pedro de Valdez was universally loved and honoured, and his desertion

in the face of an enemy so inferior in numbers
was regarded as scandalous poltroonery. Monday
morning broke heavily. The wind was gone, but
there was still a considerable swell. The English
were hull down behind. The day was spent in
repairing damages and nailing lead over the shot-
holes. Recalde was moved to the front, to be out
of harm's way, and De Leyva took his post in the
rear.

At sunset they were outside Portland. The
English had come up within a league; but it was
now dead calm, and they drifted apart in the tide.
The Duke thought of nothing, but at midnight the
Spanish officers stirred him out of his sleep to urge
him to set his great galleasses to work; now was
their chance. The dawn brought a chance still
better, for it brought an east wind, and the Spaniards had now the weather-gage. Could they once
close and grapple with the English ships, their superior numbers would then assure them a victory, and
Howard, being to leeward and inshore, would have
to pass through the middle of the Spanish line to
recover his advantage. However, it was the same
story. The Spaniards could not use an opportunity
when they had one. New-modelled for superiority
of sailing, the English ships had the same advantage over the galleons as the steam cruisers would
have over the old three-deckers. While the breeze
held they went where they pleased. The Spaniards
were out-sailed, out-matched, crushed by guns of

longer range than theirs. Their own shot flew
high over the low English hulls, while every ball
found its way through their own towering sides.
This time the *San Martin* was in the thick of it.
Her double timbers were ripped and torn; the holy
standard was cut in two; the water poured through
the shot-holes. The men lost their nerve. In such
ships as had no gentlemen on board notable signs
were observed of flinching.

At the end of that day's fighting the English
powder gave out. Two days' service had been the
limit of the Queen's allowance. Howard had
pressed for a more liberal supply at the last
moment, and had received the characteristic
answer that he must state precisely how much he
wanted before more could be sent. The lighting of
the beacons had quickened the official pulse a little.
A small addition had been despatched to Weymouth
or Poole, and no more could be done till it arrived.
The Duke, meanwhile, was left to smooth his
ruffled plumes and drift on upon his way. But by
this time England was awake. Fresh privateers,
with powder, meat, bread, fruit, anything that they
could bring, were pouring out from the Dorsetshire
harbours. Sir George Carey had come from the
Needles in time to share the honours of the last
battle, ' round shot,' as he said, ' flying thick as
musket balls in a skirmish on land.'

The Duke had observed uneasily from the *San
Martin's* deck that his pursuers were growing

numerous. He had made up his mind definitely
to go for the Isle of Wight, shelter his fleet in the
Solent, land 10,000 men in the island, and stand
on his defence till he heard from Parma. He must
fight another battle ; but, cut up as he had been,
he had as yet lost but two ships, and those by accident. He might fairly hope to force his way in
with help from above, for which he had special
reason to look in the next engagement. Wednesday was a breathless calm. The English were
taking in their supplies. The Armada lay still,
repairing damages. Thursday would be St.
Dominic's Day. St. Dominic belonged to the
Duke's own family, and was his patron saint. St.
Dominic, he felt sure, would now stand by his
kinsman.

The morning broke with a light air. The
English would be less able to move, and with the
help of the galleasses he might hope to come to
close quarters at last. Howard seemed inclined to
give him his wish. With just wind enough to move
the Lord Admiral led in the *Ark Raleigh* straight
down on the Spanish centre. The *Ark* outsailed
her consorts and found herself alone with the galleons all round her. At that moment the wind
dropped. The Spanish boarding-parties were at
their posts. The tops were manned with musketeers, the grappling irons all prepared to fling
into the *Ark's* rigging. In imagination the
English admiral was their own. But each day's

P

experience was to teach them a new lesson. Eleven boats dropped from the *Ark's* sides and took her in tow. The breeze rose again as she began to move. Her sails filled, and she slipped away through the water, leaving the Spaniards as if they were at anchor, staring in helpless amazement. The wind brought up Drake and the rest, and then began again the terrible cannonade from which the Armada had already suffered so frightfully. It seemed that morning as if the English were using guns of even heavier metal than on either of the preceding days. The armament had not been changed. The growth was in their own frightened imagination. The Duke had other causes for uneasiness. His own magazines were also giving out under the unexpected demands upon them. One battle was the utmost which he had looked for. He had fought three, and the end was no nearer than before. With resolution he might still have made his way into St. Helen's roads, for the English were evidently afraid to close with him. But when St. Dominic, too, failed him he lost his head. He lost his heart, and losing heart he lost all. In the Solent he would have been comparatively safe, and he could easily have taken the Isle of Wight; but his one thought now was to find safety under Parma's gaberdine and make for Calais or Dunkirk. He supposed Parma to have already embarked, on hearing of his coming, with a second armed fleet, and in condition for immediate action.

He sent on another pinnace, pressing for help, pressing for ammunition, and fly-boats to protect the galleons; and Parma was himself looking to be supplied from the Armada, with no second fleet at all, only a flotilla of river barges which would need a week's work to be prepared for the crossing.

Philip had provided a splendid fleet, a splendid army, and the finest sailors in the world except the English. He had failed to realise that the grandest preparations are useless with a fool to command. The poor Duke was less to blame than his master. An office had been thrust upon him for which he knew that he had not a single qualification. His one anxiety was to find Parma, lay the weight on Parma's shoulders, and so have done with it.

On Friday he was left alone to make his way up Channel towards the French shore. The English still followed, but he counted that in Calais roads he would be in French waters, where they would not dare to meddle with him. They would then, he thought, go home and annoy him no further. As he dropped anchor in the dusk outside Calais on Saturday evening he saw, to his disgust, that the *endemoniada gente*—the infernal devils—as he called them, had brought up at the same moment with himself, half a league astern of him. His one trust was in the Prince of Parma, and Parma at any rate was now within touch.

LECTURE IX

DEFEAT OF THE ARMADA

IN the gallery at Madrid there is a picture, painted by Titian, representing the Genius of Spain coming to the delivery of the afflicted Bride of Christ. Titian was dead, but the temper of the age survived, and in the study of that great picture you will see the spirit in which the Spanish nation had set out for the conquest of England. The scene is the seashore. The Church a naked Andromeda, with dishevelled hair, fastened to the trunk of an ancient disbranched tree. The cross lies at her feet, the cup overturned, the serpents of heresy biting at her from behind with uplifted crests. Coming on before a leading breeze is the sea monster, the Moslem fleet, eager for their prey; while in front is Perseus, the Genius of Spain, banner in hand, with the legions of the faithful laying not raiment before him, but shield and helmet, the apparel of war for the Lady of Nations to clothe herself with strength and smite her foes.

In the Armada the crusading enthusiasm had reached its point and focus. England was the stake to which the Virgin, the daughter of Sion, was bound in captivity. Perseus had come at last in the person of the Duke of Medina Sidonia, and with him all that was best and brightest in the countrymen of Cervantes, to break her bonds and replace her on her throne. They had sailed into the Channel in pious hope, with the blessed banner waving over their heads.

To be the executor of the decrees of Providence is a lofty ambition, but men in a state of high emotion overlook the precautions which are not to be dispensed with even on the sublimest of errands. Don Quixote, when he set out to redress the wrongs of humanity, forgot that a change of linen might be necessary, and that he must take money with him to pay his hotel bills. Philip II., in sending the Armada to England, and confident in supernatural protection, imagined an unresisted triumphal procession. He forgot that contractors might be rascals, that water four months in the casks in a hot climate turned putrid, and that putrid water would poison his ships' companies, though his crews were companies of angels. He forgot that the servants of the evil one might fight for their mistress after all, and that he must send adequate supplies of powder, and, worst forgetfulness of all, that a great naval expedition required a leader who understood his business. Perseus, in the shape of the Duke of Medina Sidonia, after a week of disastrous battles, found himself at the end of it in an exposed roadstead, where he ought never to have been, nine-tenths of his provisions thrown overboard as unfit for food, his ammunition exhausted by the unforeseen demands upon it, the seamen and soldiers harassed and dispirited, officers the whole week without sleep, and the enemy, who had hunted him from Plymouth to Calais, anchored within half a league of him.

Still, after all his misadventures, he had brought the fleet, if not to the North Foreland, yet within a few miles of it, and to outward appearance not materially injured. Two of the galleons had been taken ; a third, the *Santa Aña*, had strayed ; and his galleys had left him, being found too weak for the Channel sea; but the great armament had reached its destination substantially uninjured so far as English eyes could see. Hundreds of men had been killed and hundreds more wounded, and the spirit of the rest had been shaken. But the loss of life could only be conjectured on board the English fleet. The English admiral could only see that the Duke was now in touch with Parma. Parma, they knew, had an army at Dunkirk with him, which was to cross to England. He had been collecting men, barges, and transports all the winter and spring, and the backward state of Parma's preparations could not be anticipated, still less relied upon. The Calais anchorage was unsafe ; but at that season of the year, especially after a wet summer, the weather usually settled ; and to attack the Spaniards in a French port might be dangerous

for many reasons. It was uncertain after the day
of the Barricades whether the Duke of Guise or
Henry of Valois was master of France, and a
violation of the neutrality laws might easily at that
moment bring Guise and France into the field on
the Spaniards' side. It was, no doubt, with some
such expectation that the Duke and his advisers
had chosen Calais as the point at which to bring
up. It was now Saturday, the 7th of August. The
governor of the town came off in the evening to
the *San Martin*. He expressed surprise to see the
Spanish fleet in so exposed a position, but he was
profuse in his offers of service. Anything which the
Duke required should be provided, especially every
facility for communicating with Dunkirk and Parma.
The Duke thanked him, said that he supposed
Parma to be already embarked with his troops, ready
for the passage, and that his own stay in the roads
would be but brief. On Monday morning at latest he
expected that the attempt to cross would be made.
The governor took his leave, and the Duke, relieved
from his anxieties, was left to a peaceful night. He
was disturbed on the Sunday morning by an express
from Parma informing him that, so far from being
embarked, the army could not be ready for a fortnight. The barges were not in condition for sea.
The troops were in camp. The arms and stores
were on the quays at Dunkirk. As for the fly-boats
and ammunition which the Duke had asked for, he
had none to spare. He had himself looked to be

supplied from the Armada. He promised to use his best expedition, but the Duke, meanwhile, must see to the safety of the fleet.

Unwelcome news to a harassed landsman thrust into the position of an admiral and eager to be rid of his responsibilities. If by evil fortune the northwester should come down upon him, with the shoals and sandbanks close under his lee, he would be in a bad way. Nor was the view behind him calculated for comfort. There lay the enemy almost within gunshot, who, though scarcely more than half his numbers, had hunted him like a pack of bloodhounds, and, worse than all, in double strength; for the Thames squadron—three Queen's ships and thirty London adventurers—under Lord H. Seymour and Sir John Hawkins, had crossed in the night. There they were between him and Cape Grisnez, and the reinforcement meant plainly enough that mischief was in the wind.

After a week so trying the Spanish crews would have been glad of a Sunday's rest if they could have had it; but the rough handling which they had gone through had thrown everything into disorder. The sick and wounded had to be cared for, torn rigging looked to, splintered timbers mended, decks scoured, and guns and arms cleaned up and put to rights. And so it was that no rest could be allowed; so much had to be done, and so busy was everyone, that the usual rations were not served out and the Sunday was kept as a fast. In the afternoon the stewards went ashore for fresh meat and vegetables. They came back with their boats loaded, and the prospect seemed a little less gloomy. Suddenly, as the Duke and a group of officers were watching the English fleet from the *San Martin's* poop deck, a small smart pinnace, carrying a gun in her bow, shot out from Howard's lines, bore down on the *San Martin*, sailed round her, sending in a shot or two as she passed, and went off unhurt. The Spanish officers could not help admiring such airy impertinence. Hugo de Monçada sent a ball after the pinnace, which went through her mainsail, but did no damage, and the pinnace again disappeared behind the English ships.

So a Spanish officer describes the scene. The English story says nothing of the pinnace; but she doubtless came and went as the Spaniard says, and for sufficient purpose. The English, too, were in straits, though the Duke did not dream of it. You will remember that the last supplies which the Queen had allowed to the fleet had been issued in the middle of June. They were to serve for a month, and the contractors were forbidden to prepare more. The Queen had clung to her hope that her differences with Philip were to be settled by the Commission at Ostend; and she feared that if Drake and Howard were too well furnished they would venture some fresh rash stroke on the coast of Spain, which might mar the negotiations. Their month's provisions had been stretched to serve for six weeks, and when the Armada appeared but two full days' rations remained. On these they had fought their way up Channel. Something had been brought out by private exertion on the Dorsetshire coast, and Seymour had, perhaps, brought a little more. But they were still in extremity. The contractors had warned the Government that they could provide nothing without notice, and notice had not been given. The adventurers were in better state, having been equipped by private owners. But the Queen's ships in a day or two more must either go home or their crews would be starving. They had been on reduced rations for near two months. Worse than that, they were still poisoned by the sour beer. The Queen had changed her mind so often, now ordering the fleet to prepare for sea, then recalling her instructions and paying off the men, that those whom Howard had with him had been enlisted in haste, had come on board as they were, and their clothes were hanging in rags on them. The fighting and the sight of the flying Spaniards were meat and drink, and clothing too, and had made them careless of all else. There was no fear of mutiny; but there was a limit to the toughest endurance. If the Armada was left undisturbed a long struggle might be still before them. The enemy would recover from its flurry, and Parma would come out from Dunkirk. To attack them directly in French waters might lead

to perilous complications, while delay meant famine.
The Spanish fleet had to be started from the roads
in some way. Done it must be, and done immediately.

Then, on that same Sunday afternoon a memor-
able council of war was held in the *Ark's* main
cabin. Howard, Drake, Seymour, Hawkins, Martin
Frobisher, and two or three others met to consult,
knowing that on them at that moment the liberties
of England were depending. Their resolution was
taken promptly. There was no time for talk.
After nightfall a strong flood tide would be setting
up along shore to the Spanish anchorage. They
would try what could be done with fire ships, and
the excursion of the pinnace, which was taken for
bravado, was probably for a survey of the Armada's
exact position. Meantime eight useless vessels
were coated with pitch—hulls, spars, and rigging.
Pitch was poured on the decks and over the sides,
and parties were told off to steer them to their
destination and then fire and leave them.

The hours stole on, and twilight passed into
dark. The night was without a moon. The Duke
paced his deck late with uneasy sense of danger.
He observed lights moving up and down the
English lines, and imagining that the *endemoniada
gente*—the infernal devils—might be up to mischief,
ordered a sharp look-out. A faint westerly air was
curling the water, and towards midnight the
watchers on board the galleons made out dimly

several ships which seemed to be drifting down upon them. Their experience since the action off Plymouth had been so strange and unlooked for that anything unintelligible which the English did was alarming. The phantom forms drew nearer, and were almost among them when they broke into a blaze from water-line to truck, and the two fleets were seen by the lurid light of the conflagration; the anchorage, the walls and windows of Calais, and the sea shining red far as eye could reach, as if the ocean itself was burning. Among the dangers which they might have to encounter, English fireworks had been especially dreaded by the Spaniards. Fire ships—a fit device of heretics —had worked havoc among the Spanish troops, when the bridge was blown up, at Antwerp. They imagined that similar infernal machines were approaching the Armada. A capable commander would have sent a few launches to grapple the burning hulks, which of course were now deserted, and tow them out of harm's way. Spanish sailors were not cowards, and would not have flinched from duty because it might be dangerous; but the Duke and Diego Florez lost their heads again. A signal gun from the *San Martin* ordered the whole fleet to slip their cables and stand out to sea.

Orders given in panic are doubly unwise, for they spread the terror in which they originate. The danger from the fire ships was chiefly from the effect on the imagination, for they appear to have drifted by and done no real injury. And it speaks well for the seamanship and courage of the Spaniards that they were able, crowded together as they were, at midnight and in sudden alarm to set their canvas and clear out without running into one another. They buoyed their cables, expecting to return for them at daylight, and with only a single accident, to be mentioned directly, they executed successfully a really difficult manœuvre.

The Duke was delighted with himself. The fire ships burnt harmlessly out. He had baffled the inventions of the *endemoniada gente*. He brought up a league outside the harbour, and supposed that the whole Armada had done the same. Unluckily for himself, he found it at daylight divided into two bodies. The *San Martin* with forty of the best appointed of the galleons were riding together at their anchors. The rest, two-thirds of the whole, having no second anchors ready, and inexperienced in Channel tides and currents, had been lying to. The west wind was blowing up. Without seeing where they were going they had drifted to leeward, and were two leagues off, towards Gravelines, dangerously near the shore. The Duke was too ignorant to realise the full peril of his situation. He signalled to them to return and rejoin him. As the wind and tide stood it was impossible. He proposed to follow them. The pilots told him that if he did

the whole fleet might be lost on the banks.
Towards the land the look of things was not more
encouraging.

One accident only had happened the night
before. The *Capitana* galleass, with Don Hugo de
Monçada and eight hundred men on board, had
fouled her helm in a cable in getting under way
and had become unmanageable. The galley slaves
disobeyed orders, or else Don Hugo was as incom-
petent as his commander-in-chief. The galleass
had gone on the sands, and as the tide ebbed had
fallen over on her side. Howard, seeing her condition, had followed her in the *Ark* with four or
five other of the Queen's ships, and was furiously
attacking her with his boats, careless of neutrality
laws. Howard's theory was, as he said, to pluck
the feathers one by one from the Spaniard's wing,
and here was a feather worth picking up. The
galleass was the most splendid vessel of her kind
afloat, Don Hugo one of the greatest of Spanish
grandees.

Howard was making a double mistake. He
took the galleass at last, after three hours' fighting.
Don Hugo was killed by a musket ball. The
vessel was plundered, and Howard's men took
possession, meaning to carry her away when the
tide rose. The French authorities ordered him off,
threatening to fire upon him ; and after wasting the
forenoon, he was obliged at last to leave her where
she lay. Worse than this, he had lost three

precious hours, and had lost along with them, in
the opinion of the Prince of Parma, the honours of
the great day.

Drake and Hawkins knew better than to waste
time plucking single feathers. The fire ships had
been more effective than they could have dared to
hope. The enemy was broken up. The Duke was
shorn of half his strength, and the Lord had delivered him into their hand. He had got under
way, still signalling wildly, and uncertain in which
direction to turn. His uncertainties were ended
for him by seeing Drake bearing down upon him
with the whole English fleet, save those which were
loitering about the galleass. The English had now
the advantage of numbers. The superiority of
their guns he knew already, and their greater
speed allowed him no hope to escape a battle.
Forty ships alone were left to him to defend the
banner of the crusade and the honour of Castile ;
but those forty were the largest and the most powerfully armed and manned that he had, and on board
them were Oquendo, De Leyva, Recalde, and
Bretandona, the best officers in the Spanish navy
next to the lost Don Pedro.

It was now or never for England. The scene
of the action which was to decide the future of
Europe was between Calais and Dunkirk, a few
miles off shore, and within sight of Parma's camp.
There was no more manœuvring for the weather-
gage, no more fighting at long range. Drake

dashed straight upon his prey as the falcon stoops upon its quarry. A chance had fallen to him which might never return; not for the vain distinction of carrying prizes into English ports, not for the ray of honour which would fall on him if he could carry off the sacred banner itself and hang it in the Abbey at Westminster, but a chance so to handle the Armada that it should never be seen again in English waters, and deal such a blow on Philip that the Spanish Empire should reel with it. The English ships had the same superiority over the galleons which steamers have now over sailing vessels. They had twice the speed; they could lie two points nearer to the wind. Sweeping round them at cable's length, crowding them in one upon the other, yet never once giving them a chance to grapple, they hurled in their cataracts of round shot. Short as was the powder supply, there was no sparing it that morning. The hours went on, and still the battle raged, if battle it could be called where the blows were all dealt on one side and the suffering was all on the other. Never on sea or land did the Spaniards show themselves worthier of their great name than on that day. But from the first they could do nothing. It was said afterwards in Spain that the Duke showed the white feather, that he charged his pilot to keep him out of harm's way, that he shut himself up in his cabin, buried in woolpacks, and so on. The Duke had faults enough, but poltroonery was not

one of them. He, who till he entered the English
Channel had never been in action on sea or land,
found himself, as he said, in the midst of the most
furious engagement recorded in the history of the
world. As to being out of harm's way, the
standard at his masthead drew the hottest of the
fire upon him. The *San Martin's* timbers were of
oak and a foot thick, but the shot, he said, went
through them enough to shatter a rock. Her deck
was a slaughterhouse ; half his company were
killed or wounded, and no more would have been
heard or seen of the *San Martin* or her commander
had not Oquendo and De Leyva pushed in to the
rescue and enabled him to creep away under their
cover. He himself saw nothing more of the action
after this. The smoke, he said, was so thick that
he could make out nothing, even from his masthead. But all round it was but a repetition of the
same scene. The Spanish shot flew high, as before,
above the low English hulls, and they were themselves helpless butts to the English guns. And it
is noticeable and supremely creditable to them that
not a single galleon struck her colours. One of
them, after a long duel with an Englishman, was
on the point of sinking. An English officer,
admiring the courage which the Spaniards had
shown, ran out upon his bowsprit, told them that
they had done all which became men, and urged
them to surrender and save their lives. For
answer they cursed the English as cowards and

Q

chickens because they refused to close. The officer was shot. His fall brought a last broadside on them, which finished the work. They went down, and the water closed over them. Rather death to the soldiers of the Cross than surrender to a heretic.

The deadly hail rained on. In some ships blood was seen streaming out of the scupper-holes. Yet there was no yielding; all ranks showed equal heroism. The priests went up and down in the midst of the carnage, holding the crucifix before the eyes of the dying. At midday Howard came up to claim a second share in a victory which was no longer doubtful. Towards the afternoon the Spanish fire slackened. Their powder was gone, and they could make no return to the cannonade which was still overwhelming them. They admitted freely afterwards that if the attack had been continued but two hours more they must all have struck or gone ashore. But the English magazines were empty also; the last cartridge was shot away, and the battle ended from mere inability to keep it up. It had been fought on both sides with peculiar determination. In the English there was the accumulated resentment of thirty years of menace to their country and their creed, with the enemy in tangible shape at last to be caught and grappled with; in the Spanish, the sense that if their cause had not brought them the help they looked for from above, the honour and faith of Castile should not suffer in their hands.

It was over. The English drew off, regretting that their thrifty mistress had limited their means of fighting for her, and so obliged them to leave their work half done. When the cannon ceased the wind rose, the smoke rolled away, and in the level light of the sunset they could see the results of the action.

A galleon in Recalde's squadron was sinking with all hands. The *San Philip* and the *San Matteo* were drifting dismasted towards the Dutch coast, where they were afterwards wrecked. Those which were left with canvas still showing were crawling slowly after their comrades who had not been engaged, the spars and rigging so cut up that they could scarce bear their sails. The loss of life could only be conjectured, but it had been obviously terrible. The nor'-wester was blowing up and was pressing the wounded ships upon the shoals, from which, if it held, it seemed impossible in their crippled state they would be able to work off.

In this condition Drake left them for the night, not to rest, but from any quarter to collect, if he could, more food and powder. The snake had been scotched, but not killed. More than half the great fleet were far away, untouched by shot, perhaps able to fight a second battle if they recovered heart. To follow, to drive them on the banks if the wind held, or into the North Sea, anywhere so that he left them no chance of joining hands with Parma again, and to use the time before they had rallied from his blows, that was the present necessity. His own poor fellows were famished and in rags; but neither he nor they had leisure to think of themselves. There was but one thought in the whole of them, to be again in chase of the flying foe. Howard was resolute as Drake. All that was possible was swiftly done. Seymour and the Thames squadron were to stay in the Straits and watch Parma. From every attainable source food and powder were collected for the rest—far short in both ways of what ought to have been, but, as Drake said, 'we were resolved to put on a brag and go on as if we needed nothing.' Before dawn the admiral and he were again off on the chase.

The brag was unneeded. What man could do had been done, and the rest was left to the elements. Never again could Spanish seamen be brought to face the English guns with Medina Sidonia to lead them. They had a fool at their head. The Invisible Powers in whom they had been taught to trust had deserted them. Their confidence was gone and their spirit broken. Drearily the morning broke on the Duke and his consorts the day after the battle. The Armada had collected in the night. The nor'-wester had freshened to a gale, and they were labouring heavily along, making fatal leeway towards the shoals.

It was St. Lawrence's Day, Philip's patron

saint, whose shoulder-bone he had lately added to
the treasures of the Escurial; but St. Lawrence
was as heedless as St. Dominic. The *San Martin*
had but six fathoms under her. Those nearer to
the land signalled five, and right before them they
could see the brown foam of the breakers curling
over the sands, while on their weather-beam, a mile
distant and clinging to them like the shadow of
death, were the English ships which had pursued
them from Plymouth like the dogs of the Furies.
The Spanish sailors and soldiers had been without
food since the evening when they anchored at
Calais. All Sunday they had been at work, no rest
allowed them to eat. On the Sunday night they
had been stirred out of their sleep by the fire ships.
Monday they had been fighting, and Monday night
committing their dead to the sea. Now they
seemed advancing directly upon inevitable destruction. As the wind stood there was still room for
them to wear and thus escape the banks, but they
would then have to face the enemy, who seemed
only refraining from attacking them because while
they continued on their present course the winds
and waves would finish the work without help from
man. Recalde, De Leyva, Oquendo, and other
officers were sent for to the *San Martin* to consult.
Oquendo came last. 'Ah, Señor Oquendo,' said the
Duke as the heroic Biscayan stepped on board, 'que
haremos?' (what shall we do?) 'Let your Ex-
cellency bid load the guns again,' was Oquendo's

gallant answer. It could not be. De Leyva himself said that the men would not fight the English again. Florez advised surrender. The Duke wavered. It was said that a boat was actually lowered to go off to Howard and make terms, and that Oquendo swore that if the boat left the *San Martin* on such an errand he would fling Florez into the sea. Oquendo's advice would have, perhaps, been the safest if the Duke could have taken it. There were still seventy ships in the Armada little hurt. The English were 'bragging,' as Drake said, and in no condition themselves for another serious engagement. But the temper of the entire fleet made a courageous course impossible. There was but one Oquendo. Discipline was gone. The soldiers in their desperation had taken the command out of the hands of the seamen. Officers and men alike abandoned hope, and, with no human prospect of salvation left to them, they flung themselves on their knees upon the decks and prayed the Almighty to have pity on them. But two weeks were gone since they had knelt on those same decks on the first sight of the English shore to thank Him for having brought them so far on an enterprise so glorious. Two weeks ; and what weeks ! Wrecked, torn by cannon shot, ten thousand of them dead or dying—for this was the estimated loss by battle—the survivors could now but pray to be delivered from a miserable death by the elements. In cyclones the wind often changes suddenly back from north-west to west, from west to south. At that moment, as if in answer to their petition, one of these sudden shifts of wind saved them from the immediate peril. The gale backed round to S.S.W., and ceased to press them on the shoals. They could ease their sheets, draw off into open water, and steer a course up the middle of the North Sea.

So only that they went north, Drake was content to leave them unmolested. Once away into the high latitudes they might go where they would. Neither Howard nor he, in the low state of their own magazines, desired any unnecessary fighting. If the Armada turned back they must close with it. If it held its present course they must follow it till they could be assured it would communicate no more for that summer with the Prince of Parma. Drake thought they would perhaps make for the Baltic or some port in Norway. They would meet no hospitable reception from either Swedes or Danes, but they would probably try. One only imminent danger remained to be provided against. If they turned into the Forth, it was still possible for the Spaniards to redeem their defeat, and even yet shake Elizabeth's throne. Among the many plans which had been formed for the invasion of England, a landing in Scotland had long been the favourite. Guise had always preferred Scotland when it was intended that Guise should be the leader. Santa Cruz had been in close correspon-

dence with Guise on this very subject, and many
officers in the Armada must have been acquainted
with Santa Cruz's views. The Scotch Catholic
nobles were still savage at Mary Stuart's execution,
and had the Armada anchored in Leith Roads with
twenty thousand men, half a million ducats, and a
Santa Cruz at its head, it might have kindled a
blaze at that moment from John o' Groat's Land
to the Border.

But no such purpose occurred to the Duke of
Medina Sidonia. He probably knew nothing at all
of Scotland or its parties. Among the many de-
ficiencies which he had pleaded to Philip as un-
fitting him for the command, he had said that Santa
Cruz had acquaintances among the English and
Scotch peers. He had himself none. The small
information which he had of anything did not go
beyond his orange gardens and his tunny fishing.
His chief merit was that he was conscious of his
incapacity ; and, detesting a service into which he
had been fooled by a hysterical nun, his only
anxiety was to carry home the still considerable
fleet which had been trusted to him without further
loss. Beyond Scotland and the Scotch isles there
was the open ocean, and in the open ocean there
were no sandbanks and no English guns. Thus,
with all sail set he went on before the wind. Drake
and Howard attended him till they had seen him
past the Forth, and knew then that there was no
more to fear. It was time to see to the wants of

their own poor fellows, who had endured so patiently and fought so magnificently. On the 13th of August they saw the last of the Armada, turned back, and made their way to the Thames.

But the story has yet to be told of the final fate of the great ' enterprise of England ' (the ' empresa de Inglaterra '), the object of so many prayers, on which the hopes of the Catholic world had been so long and passionately fixed. It had been ostentatiously a religious crusade. The preparations had been attended with peculiar solemnities. In the eyes of the faithful it was to be the execution of Divine justice on a wicked princess and a wicked people. In the eyes of millions whose convictions were less decided it was an appeal to God's judgment to decide between the Reformation and the Pope. There was an appropriateness, therefore, if due to accident, that other causes besides the action of man should have combined in its overthrow.

The Spaniards were experienced sailors; a voyage round the Orkneys and round Ireland to Spain might be tedious, but at that season of the year need not have seemed either dangerous or difficult. On inquiry, however, it was found that the condition of the fleet was seriously alarming. The provisions placed on board at Lisbon had been found unfit for food, and almost all had been thrown into the sea. The fresh stores taken in at Corunna had been consumed, and it was found that at the present rate there would be nothing left in a fortnight. Worse than all, the water-casks refilled there had been carelessly stowed. They had been shot through in the fighting and were empty; while of clothing or other comforts for the cold regions which they were entering no thought had been taken. The mules and horses were flung overboard, and Scotch smacks, which had followed the retreating fleet, reported that they had sailed for miles through floating carcases.

The rations were reduced for each man to a daily half-pound of biscuit, a pint of water, and a pint of wine. Thus, sick and hungry, the wounded left to the care of a medical officer, who went from ship to ship, the subjects of so many prayers were left to encounter the climate of the North Atlantic. The Duke blamed all but himself; he hanged one poor captain for neglect of orders, and would have hanged another had he dared; but his authority was gone. They passed the Orkneys in a single body. They then parted, it was said in a fog; but each commander had to look out for himself and his men. In many ships water must be had somewhere, or they would die. The *San Martin*, with sixty consorts, went north to the sixtieth parallel. From that height the pilots promised to take them down clear of the coast. The wind still clung to the west, each day blowing harder than the last. When they braced round to it their wounded spars gave way. Their rigging parted. With the greatest difficulty

they made at last sufficient offing, and rolled down
somehow out of sight of land, dipping their yards in
the enormous seas. Of the rest, one or two went
down among the Western Isles and became wrecks
there, their crews, or part of them, making their
way through Scotland to Flanders. Others went
north to Shetland or the Faroe Islands. Between
thirty and forty were tempted in upon the Irish
coasts. There were Irishmen in the fleet, who must
have told them that they would find the water
there for which they were perishing, safe harbours,
and a friendly Catholic people; and they found
either harbours which they could not reach or sea-
washed sands and reefs. They were all wrecked at
various places between Donegal and the Blaskets.
Something like eight thousand half-drowned
wretches struggled on shore alive. Many were
gentlemen, richly dressed, with velvet coats, gold
chains, and rings. The common sailors and soldiers
had been paid their wages before they started, and
each had a bag of ducats lashed to his waist when
he landed through the surf. The wild Irish of the
coast, tempted by the booty, knocked unknown
numbers of them on the head with their battle-
axes, or stripped them naked and left them to die
of the cold. On one long sand strip in Sligo an
English officer counted eleven hundred bodies, and
he heard that there were as many more a few miles
distant.

The better-educated of the Ulster chiefs, the

O'Rourke and O'Donnell, hurried down to stop the butchery and spare Ireland the shame of murdering helpless Catholic friends. Many—how many cannot be said—found protection in their castles. But even so it seemed as if some inexorable fate pursued all who had sailed in that doomed expedition. Alonzo de Leyva, with half a hundred young Spanish nobles of high rank who were under his special charge, made his way in a galleass into Killibeg. He was himself disabled in landing. O'Donnell received and took care of him and his companions. After remaining in O'Donnell's castle for a month he recovered. The weather appeared to mend. The galleass was patched up, and De Leyva ventured an attempt to make his way in her to Scotland. He had passed the worst danger, and Scotland was almost in sight; but fate would have its victims. The galleass struck a rock off Dunluce and went to pieces, and Don Alonzo and the princely youths who had sailed with him were washed ashore all dead, to find an unmarked grave in Antrim.

Most pitiful of all was the fate of those who fell into the hands of the English garrisons in Galway and Mayo. Galleons had found their way into Galway Bay—one of them had reached Galway itself—the crews half dead with famine and offering a cask of wine for a cask of water. The Galway townsmen were human, and tried to feed and care for them. Most were too far gone to be revived, and died of exhaustion. Some might have recovered, but recovered they would be a danger to the State. The English in the West of Ireland were but a handful in the midst of a sullen, half-conquered population. The ashes of the Desmond rebellion were still smoking, and Dr. Sanders and his Legatine Commission were fresh in immediate memory. The defeat of the Armada in the Channel could only have been vaguely heard of. All that English officers could have accurately known must have been that an enormous expedition had been sent to England by Philip to restore the Pope; and Spaniards, they found, were landing in thousands in the midst of them with arms and money; distressed for the moment, but sure, if allowed time to get their strength again, to set Connaught in a blaze. They had no fortresses to hold so many prisoners, no means of feeding them, no men to spare to escort them to Dublin. They were responsible to the Queen's Government for the safety of the country. The Spaniards had not come on any errand of mercy to her or hers. The stern order went out to kill them all wherever they might be found, and two thousand or more were shot, hanged, or put to the sword. Dreadful! Yes, but war itself is dreadful and has its own necessities.

The sixty ships which had followed the *San Martin* succeeded at last in getting round Cape Clear, but in a condition scarcely less miserable than that of their companions who had perished in Ireland. Half their companies died—died of untended wounds, hunger, thirst, and famine fever. The survivors were moving skeletons, more shadows and ghosts than living men, with scarce strength left them to draw a rope or handle a tiller. In some ships there was no water for fourteen days. The weather in the lower latitudes lost part of its violence, or not one of them would have seen Spain again. As it was they drifted on outside Scilly and into the Bay of Biscay, and in the second week in September they dropped in one by one. Recalde, with better success than the rest, made Corunna. The Duke, not knowing where he was, found himself in sight of Corunna also. The crew of the *San Martin* were prostrate, and could not work her in. They signalled for help, but none came, and they dropped away to leeward to Bilbao. Oquendo had fallen off still farther to Santander, and the rest of the sixty arrived in the following days at one or other of the Biscay ports. On board them, of the thirty thousand who had left those shores but two months before in high hope and passionate enthusiasm, nine thousand only came back alive—if alive they could be called. It is touching to read in a letter from Bilbao of their joy at warm Spanish sun, the sight of the grapes on the white walls, and the taste of fresh home bread and water again. But it came too late to save them, and those whose bodies might have rallied died of broken hearts and disappointed dreams. Santa Cruz's old companions could not survive the ruin of the Spanish navy. Recalde died two days after he landed at Bilbao. Santander was Oquendo's home. He had a wife and children there, but he refused to see them, turned his face to the wall, and died too. The common seamen and soldiers were too weak to help themselves. They had to be left on board the poisoned ships till hospitals could be prepared to take them in. The authorities of Church and State did all that men could do; but the case was past help, and before September was out all but a few hundred needed no further care.

Philip, it must be said for him, spared nothing to relieve the misery. The widows and orphans were pensioned by the State. The stroke which had fallen was received with a dignified submission to the inscrutable purposes of Heaven. Diego Florez escaped with a brief imprisonment at Burgos. None else were punished for faults which lay chiefly in the King's own presumption in imagining himself the instrument of Providence.

The Duke thought himself more sinned against than sinning. He did not die, like Recalde or Oquendo, seeing no occasion for it. He flung down his command and retired to his palace at St. Lucan; and so far was Philip from resenting the loss of the Armada on its commander, that he continued him in his governorship of Cadiz, where Essex found him seven years later, and where he ran from Essex as he had run from Drake. The Spaniards made no attempt to conceal the greatness of their defeat. Unwilling to allow that the Upper Powers had been against them, they set it frankly down to the superior fighting powers of the English. The English themselves, the Prince of Parma said, were modest in their victory. They thought little of their own gallantry. To them the defeat and destruction of the Spanish fleet was a declaration of the Almighty in the cause of their country and the Protestant faith. Both sides had appealed to Heaven, and Heaven had spoken.

It was the turn of the tide. The wave of the reconquest of the Netherlands ebbed from that moment. Parma took no more towns from the Hollanders. The Catholic peers and gentlemen of England, who had held aloof from the Established Church, waiting *ad illud tempus* for a religious revolution, accepted the verdict of Providence. They discovered that in Anglicanism they could keep the faith of their fathers, yet remain in communion with their Protestant fellow-countrymen, use the same liturgy, and pray in the same temples. For the first time since Elizabeth's father broke the bonds of Rome the English became a united nation, joined in loyal enthusiasm for the Queen, and were satisfied that thenceforward no Italian priest should tithe or toll in her dominions.

But all that, and all that went with it, the passing from Spain to England of the sceptre of the seas, must be left to other lectures, or other lecturers who have more years before them than I. My own theme has been the poor Protestant adventurers who fought through that perilous week in the English Channel and saved their country and their country's liberty.

PRINTED BY
SPOTTISWOODE AND CO., NEW-STREET SQUARE
LONDON

R

For EU product safety concerns, contact us at Calle de José Abascal, 56–1°,
28003 Madrid, Spain or eugpsr@cambridge.org.

www.ingramcontent.com/pod-product-compliance
Ingram Content Group UK Ltd.
Pitfield, Milton Keynes, MK11 3LW, UK
UKHW010339140625
459647UK00010B/710